Pictorial Souvenirs

&

Commemoratives

of North America

Pictorial Souvenirs
&
Commemoratives
of North America

Frank Stefano, Jr.

Ian Henderson, Consulting Editor

A Sunrise Book

E. P. Dutton & Co., Inc. New York 1976

Dutton-Sunrise, Inc., a subsidiary of E. P. Dutton & Co., Inc.
Copyright © 1976 by Frank Stefano, Jr.
All rights reserved. Printed in the U.S.A.
First Edition
10 9 8 7 6 5 4 3 2 1

Published simultaneously in Canada by Clarke, Irwin & Company Limited, Toronto and Vancouver

ISBN: 0-87690-198-4 (cloth)
0-87690-200-X (paper)

LIBRARY OF CONGRESS CATALOGING IN PUBLICATION DATA

Stefano, Frank.
  Pictorial souvenirs & commemoratives of North America.

  "A Sunrise book."
  Bibliography: p.
  1. Antiques. 2. Souvenirs (Keepsakes)—Collectors and collecting. 3. United States in art. 4. Canada in art. I. Title.
NK1125.S78   1976   745.1'0973   75-25900

Contents

Acknowledgments

Personal thanks are extended to John H. Roth III, importer of pictorial souvenirs and the third generation to market wares carrying the JONROTH trademark. Also to Lawrence Zimmerman, from whose collection all the illustrations of World's Fair souvenirs have been obtained, and who offered critical comment on that portion of the book. Thanks are also due to Marian Skedgell for her editing and assistance.

Thanks are due as well to the British manufacturers for their help, both with information and photographs. Especially, on this side of the water to Claudia Coleman of Wedgwood, New York, and in Staffordshire to Bruce Tattersall of the Wedgwood Museum, Robert Copeland of Spode, Ltd., and Hugh Gibson of Royal Doulton.

Drawings of the trademarks on pictorial souvenirs are by Thomas Mullaney, and the photography is by Robert Riggs. Where no credit is shown regarding an illustration, it is from the collection of Ian Henderson.

Foreword

What is known about North American pictorial souvenirs? That question was posed to me by Ian Henderson after he had completed his book about pictorial souvenirs of Britain. The answer, after some thought and searching, was "Not very much." And so this effort was started.

Although souvenirs are a large, wide-ranging field, this book is concerned primarily with "pictorial souvenirs," meaning items bearing either a view of an actual scene or at the minimum the name and phrase, "Souvenir of . . ." Both Ian and I have an interest in ceramics, and that became our major area for the work.

We quickly found that the culture, style, taste, and even art of a period are all reflected in its pictorial souvenirs, through both the views found on the surfaces and the design of the wares themselves. They represent a slice of history with as much interest for the collector as Historical Staffordshire china views of the North American Continent enjoy. However, pictorial souvenir ceramic wares have two advantages as collectibles which their earlier Staffordshire brethren no longer possess: pictorial souvenirs are available and their prices are inexpensive to moderate.

Ian Henderson, besides providing the stimulus for this book, continued to gather information on pictorial souvenirs produced in Britain, but this time about those produced for sale in the United States. You may want to read the English side of the story, which is found in his book, *Pictorial Souvenirs of Britain* (London: David & Charles, 1974).

Pictorial souvenirs, on the whole, are a new field, although certain segments have long enjoyed collector interest (Wedgwood wares, R&M plates, souvenir spoons). This book is not the complete story. It is a first step. Hopefully it will serve as a springboard to bring to light more information about our country's past, as so vividly depicted in one of the most widespread and popular forms of documentary art—the pictorial souvenir.

It is also meant to entertain you while it provides the knowledge you'll need the next time you travel for pleasure or visit a flea market or antique show and wish to add a new or old pictorial souvenir to your collection.

Frank Stefano, Jr.

Pictorial Souvenirs

Pictorial souvenirs have been defined as items manufactured and sold as souvenirs which carry a view, generally of an actual scene, or at the minimum the wording "Souvenir of . . ." and the name of a city, place, or event. They are one area within the much broader field of souvenirs.

The title of this book uses two terms, "souvenirs" and "commemoratives," but at times the distinction has been difficult to make. Therefore the emphasis has been placed on the other word: pictorial. Rather than try to suggest that "souvenirs" equal "scenes," while "commemoratives" equal "events," both have been grouped together and the term "pictorial souvenir" used to include or apply to either category.

Most of this book is about pictorial souvenirs on ceramic surfaces. This is the largest field (ignoring postcards), and there are numerous examples available at moderate prices in flea markets and more and more frequently in antique shows and shops. We also cover, more briefly, several other types of pictorial souvenirs which share the twin features of large supply and low price. However, there is no coverage here of souvenirs made of wood, leather, or textiles, or of souvenir jewelry, although many of these items fall within the definition of pictorial souvenirs. Limitations of space and research time dictated their absence.

The word "souvenir" as defined by Webster is "that which serves as a reminder." That broad definition would naturally include many items of a personal or nostalgic nature, such as the lock of hair of a loved one, or a shell picked up on the beach. Our interest here is in commercial items—those pictorial souvenirs produced and marketed as souvenirs. Such items, as a separate field of manufacture, date back less than one hundred years.

Today we have become used to wide-screen movies and TV pictures in living color, but until recently few people were able to know what the rest of the country looked like. Artists' work, prints, and some photographs were available, but a pictorial souvenir of a place would also be cherished. It seems an almost universal desire to return from a trip with a picture of the place you've visited. Today, with instant-focus cameras, to say nothing of instant development, you can make your own pictorial souvenirs, but at the beginning of the century cameras were large and expensive and difficult to use. So items which had on them a representation of a place or event had a special appeal to the public.

This could be called a souvenir instinct, the desire to remember some place or event by possessing a memento purchased while there. It's like the impulse buying that attacks you in the supermarket. The price of the item is generally quite modest, so that the souvenir instinct has been felt—and satisfied—by almost everyone.

Once a souvenir was purchased, it was unlikely that it would be thrown away, although it might be "put away." As a result, there are many souvenirs around—at the back of the closet or in the attic or the basement. Look in your own home or in that of an older relative, and see what you can find. The odds are that there will be at least one souvenir, and probably a pictorial souvenir, right under your roof.

A purist might insist that the place represented by the souvenir be the place where it was bought. Somehow to buy a souvenir of the Empire State Building in Montreal or of the Golden Gate Bridge in New Orleans is not quite cricket—unless and until you become a collector of souvenirs. Then you will discover that pictorial souvenirs similar to the ones shown in this book can be found in places far distant from the scene depicted on the article.

Part I

Ceramic
Pictorial
Souvenirs

More frequently than any other type of souvenir, ceramic souvenirs are embellished with pictorial views. The ceramic pictorial souvenirs shown in this book are primarily from this century, but the concept of presenting views of America and Canada on inexpensive china and earthenware originated early in the nineteenth century. Americans seem to have long had a fondness for seeing their own landscapes and events on ceramics.

Inexpensive wares were produced in Staffordshire between the 1820s and the 1850s, when transfer-printed views of the expanding nation were mass-produced and exported to these shores. The original color was a deep blue, which caused the wares to become known as "Historical Blue China." Records of a Louisville, Kentucky, importer show that 10″ plates were imported for seventy cents a dozen in 1833. That is a little less than six cents a plate, which covered not only the production in England, shipping across the Atlantic, and then reshipment up the Mississippi and Ohio Rivers, but a profit for both the British potter and the American merchant. Volume mattered, and such wares were literally imported by the shipload.

A plate with a historic scene on it, one that might have retailed for ten cents in Louisville in the 1830s, may today command up to several hundred dollars, depending on the view and the condition of the plate. Historical Blue China has been collected throughout this century. By now most of it has moved off the market into personal collections or museums.

These wares were not made for souvenirs, but for everyday use as tableware, tea services, and sometimes toilet sets. Why mention them here?

Because the historical wares of the 1820s, of which the U.S. Capitol (Plate 1) is an example, performed the same function as our pictorial souvenirs of more recent date: to present, on an inexpensive ceramic body, a view of a place of interest. Both show a slice of history by presenting a view as it was then, and so form a historic document to be used or displayed by owners down through the generations.

While the earlier British Staffordshire is today readily accepted as a historic document, at least to date that same recognition has not been accorded pictorial souvenirs. But then Victoriana has only recently begun to be an accepted field of interest for collectors. Eventually ceramic pictorial souvenirs will gain similar acceptance.

Ceramic pictorial souvenirs were made for many towns and areas which today seem to have little if any tourist appeal. One of the reasons is that until recent years most people did not travel very far from home, and so scenes of a nearby spot had appeal. Another reason that many local scenes are depicted on ceramics is that they were used as promotional or giveaway items. The buyer who purchased a cert in amount of goods received a dish as a premium, or it might be a token of goodwill given away by a merchant in connection, perhaps, with an anniversary, dedication of a new building, or expansion of his premises. The Old Court House, School Building, or Historic Home, as shown on the pictorial jugs (Plate 2), would have been fitting subjects for souvenirs or premiums earlier in this century.

Of course, ceramics are still being offered as premiums. Only a few years ago many gas stations offered a mug or a piece of china with the purchase of a certain amount of gas.

The most common giveaway was and remains the annual calendar. At the beginning of this century some merchants gave out ceramic calendars—either plates or the much rarer calendar tiles.

The ceramic calendar tile appears to have been the idea of Jones, McDuffee & Stratton, a Boston-based importer (see American Distributors). This firm had calendar tiles made for its customers for almost half a century—from 1881 until 1929. The 4″ × 5″ tile consisted of the year's calendar on one side, with a pictorial souvenir scene on the other. They were made for Jones, McDuffee & Stratton by Josiah Wedgwood & Sons. The copper engraving for the issue of 1903 shown in Plate 3

1. "Capitol, Washington," 10″ soup plate, blue-and-white transfer. British: Ralph Stevenson, c. 1820. *Courtesy of Dr. Faith Baver.*

2. German porcelain jugs with black-and-white transfer prints. L: 3½″, "Old Court House, New London, Conn."; C: 3″, "Stafford Springs School Building"; R: 3¾″, "The Old Oaken Bucket, Scituate, Mass."

3. Engraving for 1903 calendar tile produced for Jones, McDuffee & Stratton Co., Boston, by Josiah Wedgwood & Sons. *Courtesy of Wedgwood.*

was obtained from the files of Wedgwood. Records of the Boston firm show that in 1910 "12,000 [tiles] were produced for regular customers," which is a fair indication of the size of the firm's business. These historical pictorial giveaways are today highly prized by collectors, primarily in New England. Most of the tiles that reach the market are in that area, and find buyers quickly. They may be relatively unknown beyond the East Coast.

Another ceramic giveaway calendar which had much wider distribution was the annual calendar plate. It first appeared about the beginning of the century and remained popular until the early 1920s. The standard design consisted of the calendar of the year in an artistic layout on the plate, with the frequent addition on the front of the name and address of the merchant who used the plate as a promotional piece. Merchants all over the country gave calendar plates to their regular customers. Since the beginning of the 1950s, the calendar plate has come back into style, but now it is distributed by the pottery manufacturer rather than the individual merchant. For example, Wedgwood now makes an annual calendar plate. These plates are a special type of ceramic pictorial which belongs in the so-called limited edition category.

Whether of a major tourist resort or the local trolley-car park at the end of the line, the views of North America that were transferred onto ceramic surfaces generally tell only half the story. The surface on which the picture was displayed tells the other half. By looking at the shape and design of pictorial souvenirs, we again see history: a history of social style and taste, and the way they have changed. Ceramic pictorial souvenirs represent documentary art and are a reflection of our culture. You will find, in looking at the various illustrations, that you frequently can get a feel for the age of a piece by its shape or design without regard to the scene itself. Look at the several wares (Plate 4) that have a deep cobalt-blue background. Can't you picture them gracing a Victorian sideboard or whatnot?

These also illustrate another aspect of the wares—the older ceramic pictorial souvenirs are small. This probably has to do more with ease of transport than with cost. They had to fit easily into the handbag or luggage of the traveler, or the pocket of the gentleman.

These early wares, although mass-produced, were remarkably well-made and today are generally found without chips or damage. This is true even of items that were made in shapes that could serve practical purposes, such as the cylinder jugs shown in Plate 5. But perhaps the actual reason for their undamaged state goes back to the observation made earlier—that many souvenirs are put away. Once in the bottom of a chest, they have rested safely for more than half a century.

Regardless of the view on the surface, regardless of the shape, regardless of whether souvenir, promotional, giveaway, or commemorative, the wares had to be produced and sold. Ceramic souvenir manufacturing originally was limited to England and Germany. Today many items are made in the United States, and since the 1940s Japan has been a major supplier. In a later chapter we will review the makers, but first, and primarily, the pictorial souvenir field is an American story, the story of the distributors.

4.   Selection of German-made cobalt-blue pictorial souvenirs. 2¼″ to 4¼″ high. L to R: "The Post Office, Baltimore, Md."; "Blair Hall, Princeton University, Princeton, N.J."; "State House, Boston, Mass."; "Lake Melissa, Minn."; "Newport Beach, Newport, R.I."

5.   Colored German cylinder jugs. 2½″ to 3¾″ high. L to R: "The Oval, Milford, N.H."; "Westfield Cong. Church and Bugbee Memorial Library, Danielson, Conn."; "Dedham, Mass. Fairbanks House. Built 1636."

American Distributors

Part of the American tradition is to see the possibility for a market and to develop it. Such was the situation in the latter part of the nineteenth century. The public had begun to travel for pleasure. Paid vacations began to be a part of employment benefits. The average man had a little more money, and so some entrepreneur saw the possibility of providing the tourist with a memento of his travels, a souvenir.

At the beginning of this century the United States still lacked an extensive ceramic industry, and so ceramic souvenirs had to be imported. It is difficult now to tell who gave the initial impetus: salesmen from the European potteries or the American merchants. The British had a major hold on the American ceramic market for most of the nineteenth century and were always looking for new ways to expand their trade. They undoubtedly were able to provide assistance in design and style, as well as providing the wares themselves. The Germans also had a huge china industry in the nineteenth century and were looking for ways to expand the markets for their wares as well.

The wares were marketed through a small number of American distributors. The major ones did not number more than half a dozen. Some of them developed souvenir ceramic wares as their only business; a few others made it part of their overall business as importers.

The way the distributors got their wares to market is a story in itself. Souvenirs must be sold not only to the ultimate retail customer, but also to the local merchant who handles the items. Whatever the individual town or city shown on the ceramic surface, and whether the item was meant to serve as a souvenir for the tourist or as promotion for the local merchant or as a commemorative of some event, the market is where the merchant is located. This is true whether the scene is the U.S. Capitol, Niagara Falls, Centenary Female College, Cleveland, Tennessee, or Jefferson County Court House, Fairfield, Iowa. The only area where each of these items could be expected to have appeal and a market would be in the area surrounding whatever was depicted on the pictorial souvenir.

This fact required a sales force to make direct calls on local merchants. Salesmen literally had to cover the country. One of the largest distributors, C. E. Wheelock & Co., had as many as fifteen travelers on the road during the first decade of this century.

The typical salesman for a major jobber, c. 1910, would contact the local merchant in his store and try to interest him in having some local scenes produced on ceramics for the tourist or local trade. If the merchant was convinced of the desirability of the pictorial souvenir, he would probably go over to his display of picture postcards and pick out several scenes that either were best sellers or views that he personally liked. The postcard was the source of the great majority of views reproduced, although some of the finer scenes on wares manufactured by Jones, McDuffee & Stratton were from engravings or prints produced exclusively for their own articles.

The salesman would show the merchant the standard pattern books of wares and shapes. They would discuss what the view would be produced on: a plate (plain edge, gilt, decorated border, open ribbon border), or possibly a jug, a vase, a ceramic hat, slipper, or pillbox. Colors and the quantity of each type of item would be determined.

But before this, and especially if the salesman was having difficulty making the sale, he would have been sure to point out that the merchant's own name and his town or city would be shown on each and every piece of ware ordered. This selling point is what makes many souvenir items possess double interest today. They show not only the local scene as it was maybe seventy-five years ago, but the name of the firm for whom it was produced, giving the collector information that frequently can be dated concerning the merchant who had the item made for him.

After leaving the merchant, the traveling salesman would forward the order and the postcards to his central office. From there the order would be sent to Germany or England. German wares were porcelain and made in an endless variety of shapes and style. The British, for the most part, produced only plates or earthenware bodies.

For our example, let's suppose that the postcards and the specifics of the order were mailed to the Porzellan Manfaktur in Germany. At the German plant skilled craftsmen produced steel engravings from the views on the postcards, taking into account the shape and dimensions of the surfaces onto which the views will be placed. Each engraving was then transferred to the desired porcelain body and customarily hand-painted in colors similar to those on the postcard, or ones the artisan knew would fire well.

Some eight months to a year after the order was placed, crates arrived in Cleveland, Tennessee, or Fairfield, Iowa, with the finished pictorial souvenirs such as those shown in Plates 6 and 7. Each item would bear the legend, "Made in Germany Exclusively for Steel & Johnson, Cleveland, Tenn.," or "The Fair, Fairfield, Iowa."

That is the way the business used to be conducted. Today the German market is gone, and both the United States and Japan are active producers of pictorial souvenirs.

6. "Centenary Female College, Cleveland, Tenn." German. Cup and Saucer. Saucer 5½".

7. "Jefferson County Court House, Fairfield, Iowa." 7½" hand-painted German plate.

8. Wheelock & Co. ad from Christmas 1905 issue of *Crockery and Glass Journal*.

C. E. WHEELOCK & CO., 1888–1971

C. E. Wheelock can be considered the founder of the ceramic pictorial souvenir business in North America. This firm spread souvenir and view china throughout the country and was the first to concentrate exclusively on this aspect of the ceramic import field. By the beginning of the 1900s it was the largest wholesaler of souvenir and view china in the United States.

Wheelock began business about 1888 in Janesville, Wisconsin. He then moved to South Bend, Indiana, and in 1894 incorporated his business. One of the officers of the corporation was John H. Roth, whose story follows. With incorporation, the firm expanded into wholesaling and the souvenir field. At the turn of the century Wheelock moved to Peoria, Illinois, although for a few years the location at South Bend was retained as well. The illustrated advertisement shown in Plate 8, from the Christmas 1905 issue of *Crockery and Glass Journal* indicates that both locations were in use. Some ceramic wares, it reports, "can be retailed at ten cents each."

In 1909 John H. Roth broke away from Wheelock and started his own firm. For a few years the two firms were in direct competition. But by the early 1920s, according to Frederick Bodtke, Wheelock's president for the last quarter of a century of its business life, Wheelock had ceased importing souvenir china and had concentrated on other aspects of china importing. So, if you have a piece of pictorial souvenir china with the Wheelock name on it, you can be sure it was produced somewhere between 1895 and about 1920.

Wheelock typically marked his wares with the firm's name and the name of the merchant for whom it was made. The manufacturer's name is not given, but sometimes the area in which the item was produced is recorded. That is, the piece will be marked with the word "Germany," "Dresden," "Vienna," or "Austria." A mark used by the firm was in the form of a circle (wheel) with a cross bar bisecting it (lock). This and other marks found on pictorial souvenirs are illustrated at the end of the chapter on The Makers & Decorators.

Wheelock was exclusively an importer and jobber. Like the other American distributors, the firm did not actually produce the wares, but had specific potteries in Germany and England with which orders were placed. A sample of the wares made for Wheelock in both Germany and England are shown in Plates 9 and 10.

JOHN H. ROTH & CO., 1909

John H. Roth is the oldest ceramic pictorial souvenir firm still actively in business. It is now operated by John H. Roth III, the third direct generation of management. The firm was founded by John Roth who was at first in business with C. E. Wheelock & Co., but who formed his own firm in 1909. Both jobbers were located in Peoria, Illinois, where they remained until 1970, when Roth moved his business to Florida. Roth calls himself "The Souvenir China House of America" and for much of this century has been selling wares all over North America marked with the firm's trademark, JONROTH. This firm also frequently includes the name of the local merchant for whom the item has been produced.

Roth has used suppliers in both Germany and England. (The firm also imported metal souvenirs from Japan during the 1920s. These are mentioned on page 128.) Roth's business for the most part has been ceramic souvenirs, and since the 1940s all JONROTH wares have been produced in England. The German suppliers were not renewed after the war, so if you have a souvenir with the Roth name and an indication that it was made in Germany, you know it was made no later than the 1930s.

In 1953 the Roth firm corresponded with one of their German sup-

9. Wheelock German-made items. L to R: 2½″ jug, "Yachting, Lake Geneva, Wisc."–Dresden; 6″ plate, "Delaware Water Gap, Pa."–Austria; 3½″ jug, "Berlin and Mt. Forest from Opera House Block, Berlin, N.H."–Germany.

10. Wheelock English-made items. 7½″ multi-view gray-blue plates. L to R: "Souvenir of Catskill Mountains, N.Y."; "Souvenir of Athol, Mass."

11. Steel engravings done in Germany for John H. Roth & Co. Note view upper right, which is used on plate shown in Plate 26.

pliers, trying to determine the status of the numerous steel engravings that had been produced over the years. Bauer & Lehmann, a firm located in Kahla, Thuringia, in what is now East Germany, forwarded a list of some 1400 steel engravings covering the letters "A" through "P" which that one firm had produced for Roth. On pages 15 and 16 are the places on that list that start with the letter "P." It attests to the breadth of John Roth's business, for these were the engravings done by only one of several German suppliers, and at the same time wares were also being made in England for Roth.

Look at the names on the list. The 115 towns and places cover more than 30 states, as well as Canada. Ironically none is shown for Peoria, Illinois, the firm's home town. Maybe wares of Peoria were produced by another supplier, or maybe Roth was so busy selling souvenirs all over the country that he neglected the potential business of his own home town. Examples of engravings made in Germany for Roth are shown in Plate 11.

The advertisement in Plate 12 is from the Christmas 1910 issue of the *Crockery and Glass Journal*. Roth at that time had been in his own business for only about a year. The advertisement emphasizes the range and styles of wares offered, saying, "our line is remarkable for its variety and originality. It includes extraordinary values for the ten-cent trade, as well as the most artistic hand-painted productions for the Jewelry and Resort trade." An example of wares made in Germany with the JONROTH mark is shown in Plate 13. Remember that at the beginning of the century things did sell for five and ten cents, and the original five-and-dime stores really sold nothing priced higher than ten cents.

Locations starting with the letter P, for which engravings were made by the German firm of Bauer & Lehmann for John H. Roth & Co. during the period 1909–1939:

Pacific Grove, Calif.	Pocatello, Idaho
Pahuwska, Okla.	Poe Lock, So., Mich.
Painesdale, Mich.	Poinsettia (Calif.
Palacious, Texas	Christmas Flower)
Palatke, Fla.	Polo, Ill.
Palm Beach, Fla.	Pombroke, Me.
Palo Alto, Calif.	Pomeroy, Ohio
Panama Pacific Int. 1915	Pomeroy, Wash.
Panqitsh, Utah	Pomona, Calif.
Paola, Kans.	Pompton Lakes, N.J.
Paragould, Ark.	Ponca City, Okla.
Parkland, Mich.	Pontiac, Ill.
Park Rapids, Minn.	Pontiac, Mich.
Parsons, Kans.	Port Arthur, Texas

Pasadena, Calif.
Patchoque, L.I.
Patten, Me.
Pauls Valley, Okla.
Paw Paw, Mich.
Payette, Idaho

Pella, Iowa
Pemaquid Beach, Me.
Pembroke, Ont.
Pendleton, Oregon
Penn Yan, N.Y.
Pensacola, Fla.
Pense, Sask.
Perce, P.Q.
Perry, Fla.
Perth, Ont.
Peru, Nebr.
Peshtigo, Wis.
Petaluma, Calif.
Petoskey, Mich.
Peu Mark, Md.

Philadelphia, Pa.
Phillipsbourgh, Ore.
Phoenix, Ariz.

Picton, Canada
Pierre, S.D.
Pine Bluff, Ark.
Pinehurst, N.C.
Pine Lodge, N.C.
Pipestone, Man.
Pistakee Bay, Ill.
Pittsburg, Kans.
Pittsfield, Me.
Pittsfield, N.H.

Placerville, Calif.
Plaines, Mont.
Plainview, Minn.
Plano, Ill.
Platteville, Wisc.
Plattsburgh, N.Y.
Pleasant Grove, Utah
Plymouth, Mass.
Plymouth, Mich.
Plymouth, N.H.

Port Burwell, Ont.
Port Clinton, Ohio
Port Cycle, Me.
Port Deposit, Md.
Port de Sorel, Ore.
Port Elgin, Ont.
Port Henry, N.Y.
Port Hope, Ont.
Port Huron, Mich.
Port Jefferson, N.Y.
Port Lavaca, Texas
Portaler, N.H.
Porterville, Calif.
Portland, Me.
Portland, Ore.
Portrait Henry Wadsworth Longfellow
Portsmouth, N.H.
Portsmouth, Va.
Potlatch, Idaho
Potsdam, N.Y.
Pottstown, Pa.
Pottsville, Pa.
Poughkeepsie, N.Y.
Poulsbo, Wash.
Poultney, Vt.

Prairie City, Pa.
Presque Isle, Me.
Preston, Wash.
Prellmann, Wash.
Prince Albert, Sask.
Princeton, Ind.
Princeton, Ill.
Princeton, N.J.
Princeton, Mass.
Princeton, Wisc.
Prospect Harbor, Me.
Prosser, Wash.
Providence, R.I.
Providence Bay, Ont.
Provincetown, Mass.
Pryor Creek, Okla.

Pueblo, Colo.
Put in Bay, Ohio
Putney, Vt.
Puyalleep, Wash.

12. John H. Roth & Co. ad from Christmas 1910 issue of *Crockery and Glass Journal.*

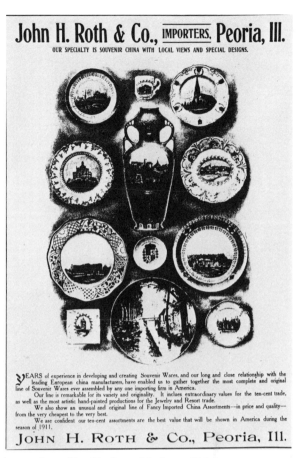

13. JONROTH German-made items. L to R: 6″ plate, "Auburn Prison, Auburn, N.Y."; 2½″ match holder, "The Old Court House, Winchester, Va."

Since the 1940s all of Roth's ceramic souvenirs have been produced in England. These carry the JONROTH trademark, and frequently the phrase "Old English Staffordshire Ware." The name of the merchant for whom the item was produced and the name of the British potter are also shown. Most articles were produced by Adams' Pottery until the 1960s, when Alfred Meakin became the major supplier. Some JONROTH items have been produced by other firms, but not many. Examples of articles made by Adams for Roth are shown in Plate 14.

14. JONROTH English-made items by William Adams & Sons, Ltd. "Lincoln's Home, Springfield, Illinois." 10″, 8″ and 6″ transfer plates. *Courtesy of John H. Roth Co.*

JONES, McDUFFEE & STRATTON, CO., 1810

Jones, McDuffee & Stratton dates back to 1810 and continues to exist today, but as a subsidiary of a larger firm and no longer in the business of importing pictorial souvenirs. However, from about 1880 through the 1940s this was *the* firm for commemorative pictorial plates. For many decades it was the exclusive agent in the United States for Josiah Wedgwood & Sons and had about 1100 different views produced which bear the Wedgwood name plus the logo "Sole Importers, Jones, McDuffee & Stratton Co."

A collector quickly learns to associate two unique ceramic souvenir shapes with this Boston importer. The first is the distinctive calendar tile already mentioned. The other is the blue-and-white transfer plate that the firm called "Wedgwood Old Blue Historical Plates." A great number of what was really one basic plate were produced, each with the same floral border but with a different historical view in the middle of the plate. By 1904, sixty-eight different views had been produced, and the total number of views is in the hundreds. The firm states that these were engraved by Wedgwood from famous paintings and picturesque etchings of historical and literary subjects for their exclusive import.

The large number of different views may have been influenced by the plate-rail feature of many Victorian dining rooms. This was a ledge or molding which ran around the walls of the room about a foot from the ceiling and on which plates were displayed. When you think of the size of most Victorian rooms, you can understand why so many different views had to be produced to satisfy the lady of the house.

The firm's advertisement in a trade magazine in 1904 stated: "We make it a condition of sale that in no instance can the plates be sold less than 50 cents each, or six dollars per dozen." By 1909 the firm's advertisements in the *Crockery and Glass Journal* called the plate "the standard souvenir plate," and the number of subjects had grown to seventy-eight different views. The price had dropped, for the copy said, "Dealers only can obtain these plates at the fixed price of $2.00 per dozen, on condition that they cannot sell them at less than 35 cents each." That was a wholesale price of under twenty cents each in 1909. These plates are on the market today at a price that runs closer to the wholesale and retail prices in dollars rather than in cents. One of these plates and the engraving from which it was made are shown in Plates 15 and 16.

Jones, McDuffee & Stratton was established in 1810 by Otis Norcross in Boston. His son of the same name later left the firm to pursue a

15. "Home of Mary A. Livermore, Melrose, Mass., 1902." 9″ blue-and-white transfer plate. Wedgwood. Imported by Jones, McDuffee & Stratton Co. *Courtesy of Wedgwood.*

16. Wedgwood engraving from which the plate was made. The text would be cut out and transfer-printed on the back of the plate. *Courtesy of Wedgwood.*

17. Wedgwood engraving for 100th anniversary of Jones, McDuffee & Stratton, Co. Again, information at the bottom would have been transferred to the back of the plate. *Courtesy of Wedgwood.*

political career that included being Mayor of Boston. The three men for whom the firm is named are Jerome Jones (he entered the firm in 1853), Louis P. McDuffee (entered in 1863), and Solomon P. Stratton (entered in 1866). In 1910 the firm published its own history, titled *A Century of Uninterrupted Progress,* in which it termed itself "the largest wholesale and retail crockery, china and glassware establishment in the country." At that time it occupied a ten-story structure at the corner of Franklin and Hawley streets. Obviously these souvenir plates were only one small part of the total business. In commemoration of that 100th anniversary, the firm had a special plate engraved by Wedgwood showing its history. The engraving used for that plate is shown in Plate 17.

ROWLAND & MARSELLUS, *c. 1893–1920s*

The way this firm marked its wares has misled collectors and dealers into believing that Rowland & Marsellus were British potters. They were not. They were a New York-based import firm. The confusion arises from the fact that the wares generally carry the firm's full name, or at least the initials R&M (by which all of their pictorial souvenirs are known today), and "Staffordshire, England," in a juxtaposition that suggests R&M was the potter in England. Most certainly, as with the other American distributors, the wares were made specifically for the firm but not by them.

Rowland & Marsellus was established about 1893 and remained in business until the 1920s. The souvenir wares (Plate 18) were but one aspect of the firm's ceramic import and wholesaling business.

18. "Souvenir of St. Louis, Mo." 10″ rolled-edge blue-and-white transfer plate. Imported by Rowland & Marsellus, New York.

Its most famous border, the fruit and flower, has a somewhat controversial history. It is a series of flowers alternating with a grouping of an apple, pineapple, and bunch of grapes around the flat or rolled edge of the plate. In an article in *Antiques* in September 1942, Morris Van Nostrand, who says he was associated with R&M for many years, states he designed the border. This fruit-and-flower border continues to be popular and has again been produced on plates that appear to be R&M but have been produced more recently by British Anchor Pottery. (More information on that firm and an illustration of the border is in the chapter The Makers & Decorators.) The collector of old Staffordshire will recognize this border as that used by the firm of Ralph Hall of Tunstall in the 1820s for a series titled "Oriental Scenery." But no matter who originated the border, it has certainly been popular for more than 150 years. Van Nostrand also relates that wares for R&M from 1898 to 1910 were made by S. Hancock & Sons (who potted at Stoke from 1858 to 1937). After 1910, he says, several other firms were used, but he does not mention the names. He recalls the time the firm received two orders for 1200 dozen each—an indication of the popularity of the plates. They remain popular and are available. During the past several years they have begun to appear at many antique shows and have developed significant collector appeal.

A. C. BOSSELMAN & CO., c. 1904–1930

A. C. Bosselman was one of the first wholesalers of a wide range of souvenirs and novelties. The New York-based importer is known to have produced postcards and pictorial glass paperweights, as well as to have had ceramic pictorial souvenirs produced in both England and Germany.

An example of the German wares made for the firm is shown in Plate 19. The firm also had a blue-and-white rolled-edge transfer plate made which closely resembles the R&M plates, so much so that you must look at the underside to see if the plate is R&M or Bosselman. The Bosselman plates were made by Ridgway (see page 70).

OTHER AMERICAN DISTRIBUTORS:

George H. Bowman Co., 1888–1932

This Cleveland, Ohio, firm imported pictorial souvenirs from Royal Doulton which generally featured a photographic likeness of the scene represented. The reverse bears the information: "The George H. Bowman Co. Sole Importers Cleveland," plus the Royal Doulton mark. A pair of plates is shown in Plate 20.

19. "Bluff House, Milford, Pa." Imported by A. C. Bosselman & Co. 4" pink-top, yellow-bottom mug. German.

20. The White House and Mount Vernon. 10" blue-and-white transfer plates imported by George H. Bowman, Cleveland. Made by Royal Doulton, England.

WRIGHT, TYNDALE AND VAN RODEN, 1818–1960s

This retail and import firm was in business on Chestnut Street, Philadelphia, until the 1960s. Through mergers, it could trace its business life back to 1818, when Peter Wright started a crockery store. During the 1830–1850 period he imported Staffordshire tableware to which he had his own name added, as well as that of the British potter. Sarah Tyndale was operating her own firm in 1844 and also had wares marked with her own name. These early wares represent today a specialized segment of historical interest which pre-dates the usual pictorial souvenir practice of adding the merchant's name on the ceramic article.

The pictorial commemorative view shown in Plate 21 is of a copper engraving of Carpenters' Hall done by Minton for the firm in this century. A whole series of these were done for blue-and-white transfer to plates similar to the Jones, McDuffee & Stratton series, but generally featuring Philadelphia or Pennsylvania themes.

21. Minton engraving from copper plate of "Carpenters' Hall." Produced for Wright, Tyndale and van Roden, Philadelphia. *Courtesy of Minton.*

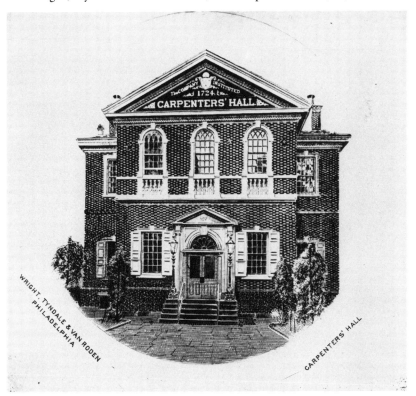

VAN HEUSEN CHARLES CO.

Earlier in this century this Albany, New York, importer had a series of about a dozen plates produced by Wedgwood in blue-and-white transfer with a distinctive floral border, as shown in illustration, Plate 22.

SHREVE, CRUMP & LOW CO.

This is a very old Boston quality store, but a newcomer to the field of importing pictorial souvenirs with its own name imprinted. In anticipation of the bicentennial, the firm had a series of twelve Boston-area views reproduced with scenes originally used by Jones, McDuffee & Stratton. The border is the same as on the older plates, so the collector must turn the plate over to determine whether the Wedgwood-made plate was imported by Jones, McDuffee & Stratton (meaning 1900 or so) or Shreve, Crump & Low (meaning the 1970s). The firm is also importing recently made tiles with old scenes, such as that shown in Plate 23. These are also made by Wedgwood.

22. "Washington Headquarters in Newburgh, N.Y." 9″ blue-and-white transfer plate. Wedgwood. Made for Van Husen Charles Co., Albany, N.Y. *Courtesy of Wedgwood.*

23. "Old South Church, Boston." 6″ blue-and-white transfer tile. Wedgwood. Made for Shreve, Crump & Low. Boston. *Courtesy of Wedgwood.*

The Scenes

The old line that a picture is worth a thousand words is as true of pictorial souvenirs as of anything else. The ceramic pictorial souvenir tells a story at several levels at the same time: taste, culture, style, as well as manufacturing and marketing techniques. Here let us concentrate on the view.

The scene on the pictorial souvenir is a moment of time captured onto a ceramic surface. These scenes could be catalogued in many ways. The presentation here is based mainly on geographic subject or activity, although, it is realized, some examples could fall into several categories.

RESORTS

The term "resort" suggests seasonal business—that is, that there is a specific period of the year when the tourist will visit a particular location. Whether you think of a summer resort at the shore or mountains or of a winter resort for skiing, it is a brief season, typically about three months in length. It is true that some places now term themselves year-round resorts, but even such locations have a "high" season. So it means that the operator of the hotel and resort facilities, to be successful, must compress a full year's business into those few months.

This is equally true of the souvenirs sold there. Perhaps a few souvenirs will be sold to off-season visitors but not many. Souvenir items must have instant appeal.

Picture Girl Scouts, schoolteachers, or a similar group getting off a chartered bus to look over the mountain scenery or to view the sea coast. Suddenly some fifty people descend on the souvenir kiosk or the checkout counter of the cafeteria. Sales will be made. And probably if one person buys an item, others will also want that item. It is the souvenir instinct in full heat, and the merchant smiles as he wraps up several more pictorial plates or souvenir spoons.

Souvenirs, from the merchant's viewpoint, mut be available in depth. That is, he wants several items that will sell, and sell quickly. He does not want the breadth of wares associated with gifts. If there were an unlimited line of souvenirs, he might never make a sale, as the customer would start to wonder which to choose—"this or that?", "whether in gray or pink?", and so forth. So he is glad to have no more than perhaps two different plates, a ceramic tile, three or four souvenir spoons, and a few other items.

The oldest resorts are in the eastern part of the United States, for that is where the nation began. Perhaps the "greener grass" theory played a major role in resort development: someone from inland New England preferred to summer on the coast, while the coast resident went to the mountains. Both areas had resorts during the past century. Travel was by rail. In fact, the railroad was a major spur to resort development, and in some cases was the sole reason for the birth of the resort.

Originally only the well-to-do traveled for pleasure, and the resorts catered to that clientele. Then, as now, there was the right time to be at the right resort. One arrived and expected to spend a certain length of time there. While there were no Olympic-sized swimming pools or dawn-to-after-dusk activities plotted by Simple Simon or the Activities Hostess, there was still plenty to keep the vacationer content. And as the person of that day might have commented, the air alone was worth the trip—whether that air was sea breeze or clean mountain ozone.

In the past twenty-five years, really a short period of time, resorts have mushroomed all over the nation. Many have been built around a golf course or near the top of a mountain for the winter sports crowd. In this recent period nationwide motel chains have developed to provide a room of exactly the same style, layout, and dimensions from one end of the country to the other.

Yet despite the changes in styles of resorts and travel, the souvenir is still considered a necessary item of purchase by anyone traveling for pleasure. Some mobile Americans don't seem happy unless they can cover all of the Northeast, South, Canada, or the whole continent on their vacation. This causes the souvenir instinct to come into play time after time as each new place is visited.

BY THE SEA

The sea has had continual fascination for the traveler, and many a pleasurable vacation has been spent on or near it. Ceramic souvenirs tell the story of these seaside resorts during much of the past hundred years.

In Maine the tourist industry, like so many others, grew with the expansion of the railroad. Bar Harbor was an early fashionable resort which still retains its charm and relaxed, almost timeless quality. Today on the island where Bar Harbor is located is Acadia National Park. The tourist might drive around Mount Desert Island and stop at Thunder Hole, which gained its name from the noise the ocean makes rushing into the spot. The illustrated view (Plate 24) is from a Spode plate made in 1957. Another older view of the area is shown in the section on churches.

Camden, Maine, has recaptured some of its past by becoming the major port for windjammer cruises. Nonetheless the scene shown on the slipper (Plate 25) suggests that the visitor settled for the motion made by the rocking chair on the porch while looking at the sea.

24. "Thunder Hole, Acadia National Park, Bar Harbor, Me." 10½″ black transfer plate. Spode. *Courtesy of Spode, Ltd.*

25. "Mt. Battie House, Camden, Me." 4½" high ceramic slipper. German.

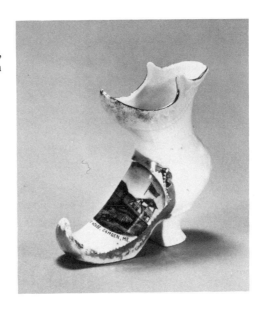

26. Pair of 5¾" German-made plates: "New County Court House, Portland, Me." (pale green border); "Portland Head Light, Cape Elizabeth, Me." (pale yellow border). Engraving was shown in Plate 11.

A guidebook titled *American Sea Side Resorts*, published in 1885 by C. Norton, provides an interesting description of other Maine resort areas. The book states, "Portland can be reached by the Boston & Maine railroad, or by first-class side-wheeler steamboat with elegant passenger accommodations. [The boats] leave Boston every evening in season." An attraction of Portland, and also Cape Elizabeth, is shown on the pair of German-made souvenirs from about 1900 (Plate 26). Norton says that Cape Elizabeth provides "a great attraction and is only 3 miles from Portland by capitol road."

Continuing down the Maine coast, Norton observed that "Old Orchard Beach gained its name from an ancient orchard of apple trees," and that the beach is called the finest in New England. It ran some ten miles in length, a hard smooth sand beach up to eight hundred feet wide. The cup and saucer in Plate 27 probably date from the beginning of the century and give some indication of the popularity of the resort.

In Massachusetts the most famous of the early resorts was Nahant, a few miles north of Boston. Its beach and early resort hotel was celebrated on Historical Staffordshire china of the 1820s. If you visualize Nahant at the north forming one claw, with Boston being the head of a lobster, then the southern claw would be formed by the curve of Nantasket Beach shown on the cobalt-blue pitcher (Plate 29) from early in this century. This beach was within easy commuting distance of Boston and was a popular day-trip spot for the whole family.

Today if the younger members of the family want to get away on their own, the odds are that they head for Provincetown at the upper tip of Cape Cod. This was the first spot where the Pilgrims set foot in the New World and has been popular with visitors ever since. The leaf-shaped dish shown in Plate 28 suggests the changes this town has seen in this century.

27. Small hand-painted cup and saucer of "Beach Looking East From Pier, Old Orchard Beach, Me." German, JONROTH.

28. Leaf-shaped dish with a handle showing "View from Town Hill, Provincetown Mass." Note the sailing ships as an indication of the age. 4½" long. German.

29. Wheelock imported 8½" plate with hand-painted view of "Fire Island Lighthouse, Babylon, L.I." Cobalt-blue jug 4¾" high of "Hotel Nantasket. Nantasket Beach, Mass." Both German-made.

Newport, Rhode Island, began to become popular as a resort after the Civil War. It reached its peak in the 1890s and 1900s, when society flowed there and built their "little cottages" by the sea. Examples of Newport's views on pictorial souvenirs are in the Glass Paperweights section, but no story of resorts would be complete without mention of this Grand Old Dame. Although many of the large mansions still stand, most have been converted into museums or are operated by church or charitable organizations. Newport still has some social graces, and Bailey Beach and the Cup Race weeks bring back some of the old grandeur.

Then there is Long Island, now home of the commuter but still an area for pleasure with the Hamptons and Fire Island. A typical Long Island souvenir is the Fire Island Lighthouse on the German-made plate shown in Plate 29.

30. Multi-view 8½″ gray-blue plate, "Views of Asbury Park, N.J." Imported by Rowland & Marsellus. English.

31. Scenes of Atlantic City. Tiny cup and saucer, Convention Hall. Oyster shell change purse with "Absecon Light House" and 3½″ miniature teapot with "Steel Pier Atlantic City."

Each vacation location along the Jersey coast has its own distinct flavor and atmosphere. In the north there is Asbury Park, founded, literally, when people pitched their tents along the beach. But they were there to have a camp meeting, and the city developed as a "haven for temperance advocates" and was named for a Methodist bishop. In the nineteenth century as many as eight thousand people a day would arrive at Asbury Park by rail, but never on Sunday. The church would not permit the railroad to stop—either to discharge or pick up passengers—on a Sunday. That was in the last century, but all through this century the neighboring community of Ocean Grove has continued to chain off its streets at midnight Saturday so that no cars can drive in the town on the Sabbath. The plate shown in Plate 30 illustrates some scenes of this resort. I am sure that this pictorial souvenir was not originally purchased on a Sunday, for the blue laws would not permit the sale of anything but necessities on the Sabbath.

New Jersey also has a city by the sea that has introduced many ideas as to what resorts should provide the visitor. Atlantic City (Plate 31) dates from the 1850s, when several promoters built a railroad to central New Jersey to serve the glass industry and saw the possibility of extending it to the shore and developing a resort. The area then was an island, with dunes and one tavern which served oystermen and traders. The railroad was built, and once again it was the golden key to growth and development. First came cottages and private homes, not like Newport's, but large rambling wooden structures with wide porches and windows. Soon some homeowners began to rent out rooms, and then hotels and boardinghouses were built. The city was on its way.

One feature which originated in Atlantic City and which it has exported to the world is the boardwalk. It was first made and used there in 1870. It was laid down at the suggestion of a conductor on the Atlantic and Camden Railroad (named, oddly enough, A. Boardman) who complained that the passengers emptied the sand from their shoes onto the train's floor. The first boardwalk was built in short sections and taken up after the season and stored indoors until the next year. But as the years went by, the boardwalk grew—in length, width, and height until now when it is some four miles long, an average of twenty-one feet above the beach and up to sixty feet wide. It is now a permanent feature of Atlantic City, as well as many other resorts around the world.

But the main reason for any seaside resort is the beach. At first people did not own their own bathing attire—they rented it. In the 1880s there were fifty-two bath houses in Atlantic City renting rooms and suits. Morals, and the law, required that anyone on the beach be properly covered. Your grandmother may have produced some shock when bloomers began to appear about 1910, and the female bathing costume included stockings until the 1920s. A woman could not show her bare legs on the beach, although some of the flappers did the daring deed of rolling their stockings down! Men also had to adhere to the proper costume, although one guidebook, dated 1885, states, "The regular bathing hour is 11 A.M., but gentlemen are allowed to bathe without costume before 6 A.M." For a few seasons in the 1920s Atlantic City employed "beach censors" who carried tape measures to insure that skirts and men's trunks were at the proper level.

The influence of the railroad is repeated again in southern Florida. Development of the whole state could really be said to have begun with one man: Henry M. Flagler. After making one fortune as a partner of John D. Rockefeller in Standard Oil, he expanded into land development and built his network of railroads down the Florida coasts. He constructed not only the railroads, but luxurious hotels, as well as planned whole new cities along the way. Palm Beach is still Flagler's golden gem.

Now although some people still arrive by rail, it is the car and plane that bring crowds to Florida. A city which has become associated with the automobile is shown in Plate 32. Daytona has long hard-sand beaches, ideal for racing. It is an apt spot to end the East Coast view of man's drive to the sea.

Any native Southern Californian would certainly hold that its beaches and resorts exceed those of Florida. California also has areas developed primarily as resorts, but the railroad did not play the major part here that it did in the East. In fact the resort shown in Plate 33 is reachable only by water. It is, according to the lyrics of the song written about the resort, "Santa Catalina, the Island of Romance." It is located some twenty-five miles off the coast of Los Angeles. The whole island was developed as a resort by William Wrigley (of chewing gum fame) in 1919. He built its only town, Avalon, with its casino, and the vacationer can enjoy fishing, boating, mountain scenery, or an underwater garden seen from a glass-bottom boat.

Another island, somewhat more than twenty-five miles off the California coast, but one also favored as a vacation spot, is the remote state of Hawaii. The illustration in Plate 34 is a copper engraving made by the British firm of Minton for a merchant on the "Big Island" of Hawaii earlier in this century.

32.   German porcelain 8½" plate with four views of "Picturesque Daytona, Fla." Scenes are hand-colored. Imported by JONROTH.

33. "Avalon Bay, Santa Catalina Island, Calif." 7½″ high vase. JON-ROTH, German-made.

34. Minton engraving of "Onomea, Hawaii, H.T." *Courtesy of Minton.*

35. A 10″ rolled-edge Rowland & Marsellus plate in blue-and-white transfer. "Souvenir of Niagara Falls."

36. "King Street East, Gananoque, Ont. Can." on a 7¾″ brown clay plate made in England.

RIVERS AND FALLS

It was called "Thunder of Waters" by the Iroquois Indians, and Niagara Falls has been a popular attraction for some two hundred years. The falls are the outlet for the Niagara River, which is only thirty-six miles long but carries a volume of water exceeding the Mississippi's. In that short length the river drops some two hundred feet in its flow (thus making rapids and fast-moving current) and almost another two hundred feet when the waters pour over the edge of Niagara Falls. The sight has inspired generations of visitors, as well as the merchants who cater to them. Probably a greater variety of items has been produced showing the Falls than any other subject. (See Plate 35.)

Traveling on the Canadian side of the border, one might have passed

37. Both items were made by William Adams & Sons for JONROTH and show views of Thousand Islands, New York, in blue-and-white transfer. Plate is 10″, jug is 3″ high.

38. 9″ openwork ribbon plate in a white glassy china with color view of "Ste Anne De Beaupré Village." Victoria, Austria.

through Gananoque, Ontario. The style of clothing and architecture in the view easily dates the ceramic plate shown in Plate 36 to the first decades of this century.

The upper end of Lake Ontario is a more recognized tourist spot. Here the Lakes stop and the St. Lawrence River begins. Alexandria Bay is the chief town of the Thousand Islands region. Some of the local sights are pictured on the ceramic surfaces shown in Plate 37.

Farther along the St. Lawrence River as it rushes toward the sea is the village on the ribbon plate illustrated in Plate 38. It was made in Germany, probably about 1920, for a French-speaking town in Canada and probably sold by an American importer to the local merchant.

39. Eight views of the covered bridges, churches, and schools in Stanstead Plain, Province of Quebec. 8¼" plate. German.

40. 2½" high ceramic hat showing "Boston & Main Bridge, Bellows Falls, Vt." German. Imported by Wheelock. (The hat says "Main" when it means "Maine.")

HILL AND DALE

Turning south through the White and Green mountains, you might have passed through the spots in Quebec Province shown on the multi-view plate (Plate 39) before crossing the border back into the United States. The Boston & Maine Railroad was one of many short-haul roads in the Northeast. Its bridge at Bellows Falls, Vermont, should not be considered an unusual subject for a souvenir. Its shape, however, as shown in Plate 40, is unusual. The hat is more commonly found in glass than in pictorial ceramic.

With the development of tourism came hotels. Some, such as the Maplewood House, were rambling structures typical of resort hotels before the motel era. This hotel, shown on a blue-and-white tile (Plate

41. A 6″ x 6″ blue-and-white transfer tile of "The Maplewood White Mountains New Hampshire U.S." The reverse shows it was imported by "A. French & Co. Boston, U.S." (The tile itself is blurred.)

42. A souvenir tea set of a size that could be used for tea for two. The creamer and sugar show "Whitcomb Summit Hotel, Mohawk Trail, Mass." while the teapot shows a "Hairpin Turn" with autos of the 1910–1920 era. German porcelain with gilt trim on edges.

41), was built in the nineteenth century in the White Mountain village of Maplewood, New Hampshire, some fifteen miles from Franconia Notch. After the 1940s the hotel deteriorated, until 1965, when, as the locals would say, there was a very successful fire. On the same site today stands a new motel type of resort with swimming pool, tennis courts, an eighteen-hole golf course, and probably by now even a new ceramic pictorial souvenir.

In the 1920s, on what is now termed the Mohawk Trail, one of the first highways was built running from the eastern states to the Great Lakes, through the valley of Massachusetts originally inhabited by the Mohawk Indians. The views on the tea set (Plate 42) show cars ascend-

43. "Grand Union Hotel, Saratoga Springs, N.Y." Wedgwood engraving used on blue-and-white transfer plate with the typical floral border. Imported by Jones, McDuffee & Stratton. *Courtesy of Wedgwood.*

ing the 2,000-foot Whitcomb summit. After coming down from the mountain, the tourist was sure to stop at a town named Florida, and just as sure to buy a pictorial souvenir, for who could resist a memento proving he had been to Florida, Massachusetts?

A still thriving resort is Saratoga Springs, New York. In Plate 43 the engraving done by Wedgwood shows one of its old hotels, long gone. In the last century the city was the socially correct spot to spend late summer. Today music and ballet at Saratoga Springs vie with horse racing and gambling as attractions for the vacationer.

To the west, one of the sights is Rainbow Falls at Watkins Glen, New York. The water and falls still attract the tourist today, but so do the rock music festivals and the Grand Prix Race Course. The plate shown in Plate 44 was hand-painted, using the entire surface of the plate, without any border left for a pattern or design.

Before the 1940s most vacationers traveled by train, and many liked to have a souvenir of the travel itself. The Baltimore & Ohio Railroad used china with scenes showing the localities through which it ran. The plate shown in Plate 45 is of Harper's Ferry, West Virginia, with a border depicting a history of the line's locomotives. In past years the plate could have been purchased in the train's dining car.

The expansion of the Chesapeake & Ohio Railroad into the Allegheny Mountains led to the establishment of the Greenbrier (shown in Plate 46) and Homestead hotels. Both were actually developed and operated by the Chesapeake & Ohio Railroad.

44. "Rainbow Falls, Watkins Glen, N.Y." 7″ hand-painted plate with the view going all the way to the border. German.

45. "Harper's Ferry, W. Va." A 10½″ blue-and-white transfer plate used by the Baltimore & Ohio Railroad in their dining cars. Made by Shenango China, New Castle, Pennsylvania.

46. "The Greenbrier, White Sulphur Springs, W. Va." 10½″ white plate decorated by Delano Studios, Setauket, New York.

The Midwest and West had equally popular resort areas. The view (Plate 47) is of Glenwood Springs near Harvard, Illinois, and is on a German plate made early in this century. The second view (below, Plate 48) is a pair of German-made plates showing Hot Springs, South Dakota. The one on the left shows the then new Battle Mountain National Sanitarium. The bare nature of the landscape suggests that this view was made soon after the Veterans Hospital opened in 1906. The building is of a warm soft reddish sandstone mined locally and from which many of the major structures of the town were built.

The view on the right shows the hot springs which gave the town its name. The pool has been in constant use since 1891 and is fed by spring water of a constant 85-degree temperature. Since this pictorial souvenir was made, the pool has been modernized and now terms itself the "World's Largest Natural Warm Water Indoor Swimming Pool."

47. "Glenwood Springs, near Harvard, Ill." An 8¾" plate made in Dresden especially for E. F. Felbeck, Harvard, Illinois. Imported by Wheelock.

48. A pair of 7" hand-painted German plates imported by JONROTH for Block & Fishman, Hot Springs, South Dakota, with views of: "Battle Mt. National Sanitarium, Hot Springs, S.D." and "Plunge Bath, Hot Springs, S.D."

49. Gilt mug with hand-painted view of "Williamsburg Bridge Plaza, Brooklyn, N.Y." 3¼" high. German.

50. Blowup of the scene on mug. Note the trolleys in the plaza.

CITIES

At the beginning of the century railroads sponsored numerous special group rates and excursions in much the same way that a group today charters a bus to visit a specific area. But no matter how one arrived, a souvenir would probably be among the things taken home from a trip to the city.

Although it is true that almost any city will have some elements of tourist appeal, and also a few items for sale as souvenirs, the number of cities that can be classified as major tourist attractions is relatively small.

The city which its inhabitants consider to be the greatest in the nation (if not the world), New York City, has numerous subjects for souvenirs, some shown elsewhere in this book. Here are two views, one expected and one perhaps unexpected.

The souvenir mug shows Williamsburg Plaza in Brooklyn in Plate 49 and 50. Before 1900 Williamsburg was a fashionable area with many large mansions. But with the opening of the Williamsburg Bridge in

1903 (which in the popular press gained the title of "the Jew's Highway") masses of immigrants previously confined to the Lower East Side of Manhattan spilled over into Brooklyn. Today the Jewish element of Williamsburg continues, for it is the center of a Hasidic community where the street scene seems timeless as you see boys with their ringlets, and men with their beards, broad-brimmed hats and plain long black coats.

The other view, Plate 51, is the world-famous scene of New York harbor and the lady who has been looking out at its activity for more than three-quarters of a century. But note here too the other views on the plate. Any pictorial souvenir will try to display the newest item of tourist appeal, and in a city like New York the view—or the absence of a particular view—helps to tell when the item was first made. This plate should date to about 1910 as it shows the Singer Building (1908) and the Metropolitan Life Building (1909) but not Pennsylvania Station (1910) or Grand Central (1913). Since 1931 two other sights have been found on many New York City souvenirs: the Empire State

51. "Souvenir of New York." 10″ rolled-edge blue-and-white transfer plate made by Ridgways and imported by A. C. Bosselman & Co.

52. "Chateau Frontenac, Quebec, Canada." Demitasse cup and saucer in black transfer made by Royal Winton (Grimwades).

53. "Cliff House & Seal Rocks." Engraving made by Minton for Nathan-Dohrmann Co., San Francisco. *Courtesy of Minton.*

Building and the George Washington Bridge. Recent decades have seen the addition of the United Nations Buildings (1950s), the Verrazano Bridge (1960s) and now the two newest features of the New York scene, the World Trade Towers of the 1970s.

A city north of New York with tourist appeal is Quebec. Its symbol has come to be the Château Frontenac as shown in Plate 52 on this cup and saucer made in England by Royal Winton somewhere between 1931 and 1950, as identified by the stamped design of the maker.

On the Pacific Coast one city is a must for the tourist: San Francisco. The two views are from engravings done by Minton some seventy years ago for the import house of Nathan-Dohrmann Co. The scene of Cliff House (Plate 53) is not the one you would find today. The present structure is the fourth (modified) building on the same site. This view is of the French château-style building erected by Adolph Sutro in 1897. It was destroyed by fire in 1907. In the ten years of its existence it was the terminal point for three streetcar lines and a popular spot for an outing. The spot remains popular today.

The other scene is of Golden Gate Park. The park covers more than one thousand acres, and like New York's Central Park, was laid out to look natural, although it was entirely man-made. The view in Plate 54 is of Strawberry Hill. Down its sides flow the waters of Huntington Falls, named after one of the men who was instrumental in conceiving the park.

A visit to the nation's capital is considered a vital part of every citizen's education, and student groups arrive in Washington by the thousands. The Capitol forms the center point or axis of the city, as laid out by the Frenchman Major L'Enfant at the end of the eighteenth century. For an earlier view of the Capitol (without its dome or wings) see page 5.

The three views shown here (Plate 55) are from this century and form a sample of the wares on which the scene is found. The mug on the left is Japanese and modern; the plate British, from the 1930s (it was made especially for Woodward-Lothrop, Washington's large department store), and the jug on the right is German, probably made during the first quarter of this century.

54. "Strawberry Hill" in Golden Gate Park. Another engraving made by Minton for Nathan-Dohrmann Co. *Courtesy of Minton.*

55. Views of the U.S. Capitol, Washington, D.C. L to R: 5½" relief mug, hand-tinted—Japan; 10½" purple transfer plate—Mason's Ironstone China; 3¾" colored view on jug by Victoria porcelain—Austria.

HISTORICAL

Almost any view has some element of history associated with it, from the local memento which may seem frivolous in retrospect, to items of dramatic and dynamic national concern. Here are a few items which reflect the founding and development of the nation: from the first colony at Jamestown, Virginia (Plate 56), to the elegance of the later Colony of Virginia as reflected in Williamsburg, Virginia (Plate 57); from the Congressional Congress at Independence Hall in Philadelphia (Plate 58) to the resultant battle for nationhood as typified by Valley Forge (Plate 59); to the residences of two Presidents, Jefferson and Washington (Plates 60 and 61).

56. "The Old Church Tower, Jamestown, Va." 10½" blue-and-white transfer plate. Adams.

57. Views of Williamsburg, Virginia. Both items are from Adams and carry the JONROTH mark and "Old English Staffordshire Ware." Plate 10". Large farmer's-size cup and saucer. Both pink. *Courtesy of Mary Aykroyd.*

58. Independence Hall, Philadelphia. 10″ blue transfer. Buffalo Pottery.

59. Views of Valley Forge, Pennsylvania, produced by Adams (plate) and Royal Winton (salt and pepper shakers) for JONROTH. Plate is 10″ pink transfer; salt and pepper are hand-colored.

60. A 10½″ purple transfer plate of Monticello. Produced for the Charlottesville Hardware Company, Charlottesville, Virginia.

61. Another 10½″ purple transfer plate, this one issued in commemoration of "George Washington Bicentenary Memorial Plates 1732–1932," showing Mount Vernon. One of a series produced by Crown Ducal.

COMMEMORATIVE

Generally the sponsors of a commemorative event will want to "do it right," so that commemorative articles are typically of good quality as long as sufficient time has been allowed for the item to be specially created and marketed. Remember that as much as a year may be required for special orders made in England, although U.S.A. manufactured items can be produced in a shorter period.

Time is also important in regard to the distribution and sales. The event may be of short duration, perhaps a week or month. The appeal of a commemorative item is severely limited after the event has passed. As the saying goes, nothing is so stale as yesterday's news. But here quality will pay off, for examples such as those shown here (Plates 62 to 67) continue to have appeal long after the event for which they were originally produced.

62. 10½" plate with a view of "The City Hall and Court House, Kansas City, Mo." Done in 1949 by Spode exclusively for T. M. James & Sons, Kansas City, Missouri. *Courtesy of Spode, Ltd.*

63 and 64. Two views of an 8″ pitcher with blue slip sax and low relief decorations in ivory commemorating "The Chicago Fire." Done by Spode in the 1890s for Burley & Co., Chicago, Illinois. *Courtesy of Spode, Ltd.*

65. "Mayflower Loving Cup." 8″ high. Five hundred were manufactured in 1970 by Royal Doulton to commemorate the 350th anniversary of the sailing of the *Mayflower* from Plymouth. Price at the time of production was fifty pounds sterling. *Courtesy of Royal Doulton.*

66. 10½" blue printed plate of "Springfield Massachusetts Tercentenary 1636–1936." Made by Spode for Hall Galleries of Springfield, Massachusetts. *Courtesy of Spode, Ltd.*

67. 7" high "George Washington" jug. Earthenware olive green slip decorated with applied ivory relief motifs. Done for Washington's bicentennial. *Courtesy of Spode, Ltd.*

CHURCHES

The display of churches on ceramics for the North American trade goes back to the 1820s, when some churches were depicted on what is now called Historical Staffordshire china. In some cases these wares provide the only pictorial records of what the churches looked like. However, these early wares were produced without any thought of selling them to the church's community or to the congregation.

Along about the beginning of this century some parishioners, perhaps at the instigation of their minister, got the idea of commemorating an individual church, or event in the church's history, on some specifically created product. Initially, the item might not have been ceramic; for instance, the Glass Paperweights section shows an example of a church paperweight. But soon the ceramic pictorial plate came to dominate the field.

Churches found they could raise funds for projects or activities by the sale of plates. They have become increasingly popular in recent decades, and the President of World Wide Art Studios (see The Makers & Decorators) says that since the 1940s his firm has "reproduced pictures of 25,000 different churches, court-houses, centennial and bicentennial scenes" onto ceramics. Most such wares are domestically produced, and World Wide is one of the major producers. However, some items are ordered from overseas firms when there is enough time and the firm is willing to supply the small quantity that such a special order might entail.

Here are some representative pieces on which churches are shown (Plates 68 to 72). The older items were probably produced as souvenirs of the town or area, rather than at the direction of the specific church. The Minton tile would also fall under that category as it has historical interest. But the plates produced in the United States certainly originated at the request of the church shown on the surface.

There are many makers of such plates today, but a large proportion of the output is concentrated in a few firms which have a wide range of decorative styles and ceramic blanks to choose from. They form a part of the pictorial souvenir field which enjoys a particular collector appeal.

EDUCATIONAL INSTITUTIONS

Schools and colleges are a bountiful source of souvenirs. Some items are produced primarily for the students, while others are meant for the alumni, parents, or the larger community around the educational institution.

While in school, the student may be involved in the pictorial souvenir

68. Two German-made articles produced early in this century with views of churches of Maine: L to R: 2¾″ cobalt-blue jar. "Catholic Church, Bar Harbor, Me."—Wheelock/Dresden mark; 3¼″ brown jug. "St. Mary's-of-the-Isle, Dark Harbor, Me."—Unidentified M/W mark.

69. Pull from a copper engraving at Minton's plant in Stoke, England, showing "First Church Quincy, Mass." *Courtesy of Minton.*

70. Articles produced in Germany early in this century, showing: L to R: 6″ gilt-edged dish "Temple, Onset, Mass." Made for R. D. Sprout, Onset, Mass.; 6″ plate with extra art work and view of "Central Baptist Church, Middleboro, Mass." Made for J. G. Doan, Middleboro, Massachusetts.

71. Pair of American-produced church plates, each 10″: L to R: "Bethlehem Presbyterian Church, Philadelphia, Pa." Made by Edwards China & Glassware Co., Rock Hill, Md; "New Goshenhoppen United Church of Christ, East Greenville, Pa." Made by L. Elkinton Lazelere, New Britain, Pennsylvania.

72. Two additional styles of American-produced 10″ diameter plates: L to R: "Canton Methodist Church, Woodland, Del." Decorated by Delano Studios, Setauket, Long Island; "First Amwell Presbyterian Church, Reaville, N.J." Decorated by Clay Decorating Studio, Hamilton Square, New Jersey.

field whenever he purchases a sweat shirt, a patch for his jacket or book, a pennant for the wall, a lamp shade, a wastebasket: all of them may carry a scene of the school. In the ceramic area, the student may buy a beer mug or perhaps a coffee cup with the name, seal, or scene of his school, fraternity, or club.

In the past, high-quality wares have been produced, frequently in sets, at the request of the educational institution itself, or some alumni group, for sale to alumni or general visitors. As with church plates, these may have been a fund-raising venture.

Plates 73 to 79 show a range of styles and designs with scenes of educational institutions. Harvard University is undoubtedly the leader in the ceramic pictorial field, having had four separate series of twelve items each produced through Jones, McDuffee & Stratton Co. and Wedgwood in this century.

The German-made high-school souvenirs show the change in educational patterns. These were done early in this century when high school was the last stop in education for the great majority of the population. A view of the high school undoubtedly had more sentimental appeal then than it has today. As with the older views of churches, some high-school souvenirs were probably ordered by local merchants rather than by the school itself.

Educational institutions are an interesting specialized field, and one in which the quality, both of the ceramic body and of the pictorial representation, is generally high.

73. "The United States Naval Academy in 1858." One of a series of twelve plates produced by Wedgwood for the sole import of Jones, McDuffee & Stratton Co. *Courtesy of Wedgwood.*

74. West Point also had a similar series of twelve views produced by Wedgwood in 1933. *Courtesy of Wedgwood.*

75. A view of Harvard University on a 5″ deep, 12″ diameter bowl. Harvard has had more than four dozen special items produced for them by Wedgwood for exclusive import by Jones, McDuffee & Stratton. *Courtesy of Wedgwood.*

76. 10″ plate with raised patrician border and view of "Wesleyan College. First Chartered College for Women 1836." Three views were produced in 1936 by Wedgwood for Jones, McDuffee & Stratton. *Courtesy of Wedgwood.*

77. "Panorama View 1935. University of California, Berkeley Campus." One of a dozen views produced by Wedgwood. 16" plate. *Courtesy of Wedgwood.*

78. L to R: "The Library, Morningside 1912." One of the twelve "Columbia Plates" also made by Wedgwood and imported by Jones, McDuffee & Stratton; "Snell and Hitchcock Halls 1931" on a series of plates made by Spode for the University of Chicago. Both are 10½" plates, Columbia in blue transfer, Chicago in gray-black transfer.

79. Two German-manufactured articles with views of high schools: L to R: pillbox with scene of high school, Allentown, Pennsylvania; 3½" high jug "Boy's High School, Reading, Pa."

The Makers & Decorators

BRITISH MANUFACTURERS

The production and importation from England of pictorial souvenirs was but a continuation of a ceramic trade that dated back to the early years of this country. The thirteen states first imported Liverpool wares: black transfer-printed jugs, mugs, bowls, plates, and pitchers during the decades from the late eighteenth into the nineteenth century. These wares featured pictorials relating to military and naval history, commerce and trade, politics, people, places, and commemorative events. These were followed by the mass production of transfer Staffordshire with literally hundreds of scenes of buildings, people, and commemorative events. These views on "Historical China" provide a unique record of North American scenery and events during the years 1820 to 1850. The Staffordshire wares themselves provided the tableware, tea services, and toilet sets for many people during that period. They were first produced in deep cobalt-blue, but later softer, paler colors were introduced until interest in pictorial ceramics declined about mid-century.

Pictorials on earthenware ceased about 1850, but England's hold on the ceramic business remained. Probably as a result of the Centennial in 1876, there was a resurgence of interest in seeing views of the country preserved on ceramic surfaces. Some items of a souvenir nature were produced by British potters for the Centennial in Philadelphia. But the real rage for pictorial souvenirs did not occur until the 1890s. That was when Jones, McDuffee & Stratton commissioned Wedgwood to produce quality commemorative and souvenir items for the American market. In some ways it is strange that Wedgwood should have been the firm chosen, for Wedgwood had not produced any of the earlier pictorials destined for these shores. However, throughout this century Wedgwood has been a very active producer of quality items for the souvenir and commemorative markets.

The major part of the British pottery industry is centered in Staffordshire, a county slightly inland and south of Liverpool, whose port facilities have been used for the export of the ceramic products. One section of Staffordshire is made up of several towns collectively known as "The Potteries," where the greater portion of all British ceramics is produced. The towns, running from north to south, are: Tunstall, Longport, Burslem, Cobridge, Hanley, Stoke, Fenton, Longton, and Lane End. Geographically, they cover a distance of no more than about fifteen miles from one end to the other. But during the past one hundred years or more these towns have spawned literally hundreds of potters, most of them small. Some ceased operation after a few years, many merged or changed names, and a few have grown into the giant conglomerates of today (ironically, many are now American owned). Name changes or changes in the method or design of marks are detailed by G. Godden in his work *Encyclopedia of British Pottery and Porcelain Work* (New York: Crown, 1964) and help to identify by whom, if not when, a particular item was made. The British, generally, have consistently marked their wares with the name or mark of the potter. Regretfully, this concern with identity does not extend to records, for frequent changes of ownership and location have resulted in the loss of documents. As a result, information on the different views, or the sources used for those views, is sketchy, to say the least.

Numerous copper engravings may still remain in storage somewhere, although many may have been discarded or scrapped for the metal content. We are equally ignorant about the names of the engravers without whose skill we would have very few pictorial souvenirs.

Pictorial ceramic souvenirs produced in England after 1891 are marked "England" or "Made in England." It was in that year that the United States passed the McKinley Tariff Act, which required the country of origin to be shown on wares that were imported.

The pictorials produced in England are almost always of earthenware and generally transfer-printed. British souvenirs and commemoratives are, for the most part, plates. The quality of this transfer-printed ware has been excellent, and there is no doubt that in time it will rival the earlier Staffordshire pieces as "historical documents."

The following list of twenty-three British potters identified with the ceramic pictorial souvenir field with North America is certainly not complete. Perhaps you will be able to add another maker or mark to the list with an example you own or have seen. Remember that the British continue today to produce pictorial souvenirs for these shores.

Where a trademark rather than the actual name of the potter is found on his wares, the maker's name follows the name used on the company's products. Marks found on the British-made articles illustrated are reproduced on pages 92 and 94. These marks are only some of those that you may encounter.

WILLIAM ADAMS & SONS, TUNSTALL

The Adams pottery was "Established 1657," according to the mark shown on their pictorial souvenirs. But confusion is immense, not only because Adams is a common name, but because there were three potters named "William Adams" potting at the same, or during overlapping periods in the past two centuries. Suffice to say that Adams is one of the oldest potteries and no newcomer to the production of landscapes for North America, as the firm produced a number of views in the lighter colors of Staffordshire during the 1830s in a series called "American Views." In this century pictorial souvenir views have been produced at Greenfield & Greengages Potteries in Tunstall, one of several locations operated by William Adams & Sons. John H. Roth & Co. used Adams as his major British supplier from 1910 until the mid-1960s. At that time Adams became a part of the Wedgwood group, and although the firm remains in the ceramic business, it has ceased producing pictorial souvenir items. Many of the wares Adams did produce were blue-and-white transfer earthenware and on Roth's items carried the phrase "Old English Staffordshire Ware." Examples of Adams-Roth items are shown page 39.

FRANK BEARDMORE & CO., FENTON

This firm was in business only from 1903 to 1914, but during that period, which saw the peak of the first wave of enthusiasm for pictorial souvenirs, it produced views for at least one American distributor. The example shown in Plate 80 is a gray-blue earthenware plate imported by George H. Bowman Co. of Cleveland, Ohio.

BRIDGWOOD & SON, LONGTON

Pictorial souvenirs were produced by this firm for the Columbian Exposition of 1893 in Chicago, and an example of a bone dish is shown in Plate 121. The firm's distinctive mark on that dish is depicted on page 94. More recent marks by Bridgwood & Son have been close in style to those of its Longton neighbor, the British Anchor Pottery Co. Ltd. Bridgwood produces wares at British Anchor Pottery, and both Bridgwood and British Anchor Pottery employ an anchor in their current trademarks.

BRITISH ANCHOR POTTERY CO. LTD., LONGTON

British Anchor goes back to 1884. It is of interest here because of its "reissue" of views earlier used on Rowland & Marsellus plates. The border is the same distinctive fruit and flower and the blue-and-white transfer is of a similar clear deep quality as the earlier ware, but the mark shows British Anchor. On the example shown in Plate 81 the back stamp is one which, according to Godden, has been in use by this firm only since 1945, or much more recently than the wares of R&M, which belong to the first decades of this century.

80. 9¼" gray-blue plate "Washington Headquarters, Newburgh, N.Y." Manufactured by Frank Beardmore & Co. for George H. Bowman Co.

81. The plate has the favorite fruit-and-flower border which had been used in the 1820s by Ralph Hall and at the beginning of this century by Roland & Marsellus on wares they imported. This view of "National Monument to the Forefathers" was made by British Anchor Pottery since 1945. It is a 10" deep blue plate. The 2¾" turned-in jug (its handle is hidden) is in brown transfer and was made by W. H. Goss.

THOMAS CONE LTD., LONGTON

Established in 1892, this firm marked its wares with its name and the term "Royal Alma." The example illustrated in Plate 82 is a plate which was produced "Exclusively for Gimbel Brothers" and is in a curved edge style, but lacks the deep roll of the R&M or other earlier styles. The color is a brown transfer, and it probably belongs to the 1930s.

CROWN DUCAL (A. G. RICHARDSON & CO. LTD.), TUNSTALL

The mark "Crown Ducal" is one which Godden says was used by A. G. Richardson, who started business in 1915 and continued under that name until 1934. A sample of the pictorial souvenirs made by this firm is shown in Plate 61. The plate, showing Mount Vernon, was made toward the end of the firm's existence, as the back reads, "George Washington Bicentennial Memorial Plates 1732–1932."

ROYAL DOULTON, BURSLEM

This firm was granted the right in 1901 to add Royal to its name for the outstanding work in the art pottery field it had produced at its Lambeth, London, studio during the nineteenth century. Its original wares were decorated by artists whose names or initials appear on the completed work of art.

The colorful figurines and family of character Toby mugs by which we mainly know the firm today are a twentieth-century addition. But the firm also engaged in the commemorative field, producing some high-quality wares, such as the limited edition jug (Plates 83 and 84) done in 1932 for the same George Washington Bicentennial as the Crown Ducal article. The artist who did the design for the Doulton jug (his name can be seen below the names of the signers of the Declaration of Independence) was C. J. Noke, the Royal Doulton art director. Note the interesting flag handle of the jug. Only 1,000 were produced, so this is a souvenir you are unlikely to find on the market.

Royal Doulton over the years has also done the more typical pictorial souvenir plate. The Bowman Company of Cleveland was an importer of Doulton items, and examples are shown in the American Distributors section.

FOLEY CHINA (WILEMAN & CO.), FENTON

The name of the pottery at which wares were made was Foley Pottery, and the name carried through as a trademark used by Wileman & Co. from 1895 until 1925. Besides the term "Foley China," wares

82. "Souvenir of Milwaukee" with side views and "City Hall" in center position in brown transfer. Made exclusively for Gimbel Brothers by Royal Alma (Thomas Cone Ltd.).

83 and 84. Two views of one of a limited edition of 1000 jugs commemorating George Washington, produced by Royal Doulton in 1932 for the bicentennial of his birth. Note the flag handle and the signatures on the Declaration of Independence. *Courtesy of Royal Doulton.*

were also marked with a crown and the initial "W" interwoven with "C." The church dish shown in Plate 85 was produced especially for "The T. Eaton Co., Ltd. Toronto."

WALLIS GIMSON & CO., FENTON

W. Gimson & Co. had only a brief business life, from 1884 until 1890, which allows us to date precisely any pictorial souvenirs bearing this firm's name. The example illustrated in Plate 86 carries the information that it was issued "On the occasion of the Prince of Wales' visit," which he made to Toronto in 1884. The insert medallion print shows the future King. Royalty is a special area of the commemorative field which has long been collected by the British, as well as by many collectors in North America.

WILLIAM HENRY GOSS, LTD., STOKE

This was the largest producer of small-sized ceramic souvenirs. Most of their production was intended for the home trade, but they produced some views of North America, such as the Niagara Falls scene shown on the small jug (Plate 81). This firm pioneered in the introduction of these smaller items. The wares were unlike most other British articles in that they were of porcelain and in a great variety of shapes: small jugs, mugs, vases, jars. They are not copies of German-made wares, but form a separate field unto themselves. They are now highly collectable on both sides of the ocean. The Goss trademark includes a falcon, for the wares were made at a pottery called the Falcon Pottery in Stoke until 1934.

JOHNSON BROS., HANLEY

Johnson Brothers represents a throwback to the last century in one type of ware that it produces. Besides making what could be called "regular" pictorial souvenirs, such as are shown in most of the illustrations of this book, it also has marketed complete dinnerware sets with scenes of this nation. This series entitled "Historic America" was marketed during the 1960s. A dinner plate with an old view of Boston Harbor is shown in Plate 87. The border of acorns and leaves is one that was originally used by Ralph Stevenson, who produced views of this nation on dinnerware some 150 years earlier, during the 1820s. It suggests that Johnson Brothers has come full circle, for the first views of the new nation produced by Stevenson and other Staffordshire potters for these shores were for everyday table use, not souvenirs. Pieces from this Johnson Brothers dinnerware service are already collectables. In several generations they could be as highly priced as the older Historical Staffordshire.

Johnson Brothers is now a part of the Wedgwood group, but it con-

85. "Metropolitan Church, Toronto." Diamond-shaped dish made by Foley China.

86. "University of Toronto" with a medallion print of the Prince of Wales on a 9½" octangular plate. Reverse shows "On the occasion of the Prince of Wales visit." Wallis Gimson & Co.

87. The 9¾" plate is part of a dinnerware service named "Historic America," made by Johnson Brothers during the 1960s. The view is Boston Harbor, and the border style was originally used in the 1820s by Ralph Stevenson. The porcelain jug shows a view of "Trefry House, Digby, N.S." and was made by Royal Century, Warwick, England.

tinues to produce and market wares under its own name and to follow the British tradition that the American shores are a good marketplace for ceramics.

MASON'S, LANE DELPH

Mason's is now also a part of the Wedgwood group, but the firm is still producing ironstone, for which its name became synonymous in the last century. The story goes that the original firm went bankrupt in the 1840s because it made such a good product there was no replacement market.

Today they make some items in the souvenir pictorial field, and the plate of the U.S. Capitol in the Historical Scenes section was from Mason's.

ALFRED MEAKIN, TUNSTALL

There are two separate Meakin firms, and their names (as with the Adamses mentioned earlier) cause confusion as to which is which. Alfred Meakin was founded in 1875, and in the past decade has been producing pictorial souvenirs for John H. Roth & Co., such as the example shown in Plate 88. The firm is now American owned, being a part of the Interpace Corp. of New Jersey.

J. & G. MEAKIN, HANLEY

The "other" Meakin is located in Hanley, some eight miles south of Alfred at Tunstall, and has been taken over in the past decade to become still another member of the Wedgwood group. It continues to produce under its own name and is in competition with its "brother" firm of Johnson Brothers by also producing full tableware services for this nation with views of the country on their surface. Two major department stores offer patterns under their own labels although produced by J. & G. Meakin. In addition the firm markets directly a dinnerware service called "American Legend"—several articles of a place setting are shown in Plate 89.

MINTON, STOKE

Although the firm dates back to 1793, any pictorial souvenir which you find bearing this firm's name will probably be marked "Mintons." The "s" was added in 1873. They have been known for superior-quality wares in many areas of the ceramic field. The firm did both plates and tiles for the pictorial souvenir business, such as the tile which would have been produced from the engraving shown in Plate 90. They also produced a series of plates for Wright, Tyndale and van Roden, mentioned in the American Distributors section.

This firm is now controlled by Royal Doulton but continues to produce wares under its own name.

88. "Historic Boston" is a 10″ blue transfer plate produced since 1965 for JONROTH by Alfred Meakin. The reverse shows an outline of a bean pot and a large letter "B" from which three lines radiate, reading "oston, aked, eans."

89. Portions of a tableware setting named "American Legend" now being produced by J & G Meakin. *Courtesy of J & G Meakin.*

90. "Old Stone Mill, Newport, R.I." Pull from a copper engraving produced for E. P. Allan, est. 1831, Newport, Rhode Island by Minton. *Courtesy of Minton.*

RIDGWAY, SHELTON & HANLEY

The Ridgway family of potters goes back to the early 1800s and with various partnerships were responsible for producing much historical china during the first half of the nineteenth century. The firm since 1955 has been a member of the Royal Doulton group. It has produced a number of souvenir items for this market, some of them on a brownish earthenware body with a fine glaze. But the item illustrated is one which might be considered an R&M plate. It is in the same deep blue with rolled edge found in plates imported by Rowland & Marsellus. The example shown in Plate 91 was produced by Ridgway and imported by A. C. Bosselman & Co.

ROYAL WINTON (GRIMWADES, LTD.), HANLEY

This firm's wares are marked "Royal Winton" and it has produced earthenwares since 1866 in Hanley at a potting works called the Winton Works. It has made pictorial souvenirs for both the United States and Canada. The salt and pepper shakers with views of Valley Forge (Plate 59) were produced for John H. Roth & Co., and the firm also did the Quebec cup and saucer shown in Plate 52.

SPODE, LTD., STOKE

Quality has been the unwritten middle name at Spode. The firm, founded by Josiah Spode in 1770, has produced ceramics at the same location in Stoke for more than two centuries. Copeland took over in 1833 but has never dropped the Spode name, and now trades solely under the name of Spode, Ltd.

A pattern book of the firm shows that more than four hundred views of a pictorial souvenir or commemorative nature have been produced since 1936. A sample of those views is the Pittsburgh plate shown in Plate 92, or the items shown in the Commemorative section. The firm has been a close rival of Wedgwood in many lines of ceramics, as can be noted from the relief pitcher of Chicago (Plates 63 and 64) or the college plate of the University of Chicago (Plate 78).

SWINNERTONS, HANLEY

A new potter by British standards, Swinnertons was established in 1906. It seems to have made a habit of changing its back stamp on wares every decade or so, which, using Godden's information, makes it simple to determine that the plate shown in Plate 93 was made after 1946. Once again it depicts our most popular tourist attraction. One could probably build an entire collection of Niagara Falls items alone.

91. "Souvenir of Plymouth, Mass." 9¾" rolled-edge blue transfer plate made by Ridgway for A. C. Bosselman & Co., New York importer.

92. "Golden Triangle, Pittsburgh," a 10½" black transfer plate done in May 1967 from an engraving by Frank Boothby by Spode. *Courtesy of Spode, Ltd.*

93. "Niagara Falls." 9¾" brown transfer plate made by Swinnerton's with a mark showing it was produced since 1946.

TUSCAN CHINA (R. H. & S. L. PLANT LTD.), LONGTON

This is another firm which has used the name of the potting works at which its wares were produced as its trademark. The firm has potted at the Tuscan Works in Longton since 1898 and is now a part of the Wedgwood group. The example shown in Plate 94 is distinctive among British-made souvenirs, for it is porcelain rather than the typical earthenware.

94. "United Baptist Church Lower Argyle NS." A hand-painted 7″ porcelain plate made by Tuscan China c. 1907.

WEDGWOOD, ETRURIA & BARLASTON

This firm is so well-known that anything addressed to Wedgwood, England, would probably arrive without delay. The firm dates back to 1759 when it, like Spode, was founded by a man whose first name was Josiah, and also like Spode, it has always been known for the quality of the wares produced. Wedgwood has always marked its wares, and although there are items that may look like Wedgwood, the axiom is that "If it is not marked Wedgwood, it is not Wedgwood." Remember, there is another Wedgwood firm located at Tunstall that is not related to the Josiah Wedgwood firm but is frequently mistaken for it. That firm includes "& Co." on its marks.

Wedgwood has continually produced quality pictorial souvenirs and commemoratives for this country for almost a century. Although other types of Wedgwood were shipped to these shores during much of the nineteenth century, this firm did not produce any of the earlier flood of Historical China. Maybe this had something to do with the way

Wedgwood entered the field of presenting landscapes on ceramic surfaces. In 1773 for the Empress Catherine of Russia Wedgwood created what probably remains the greatest collection of landscapes ever produced on ceramics. The set was decorated with more than 1,200 views of England. Although an artistic success, it was clearly a financial disaster. That experience may have restrained Wedgwood for the next century while other British firms exported massive quantities of pictorial transfer wares to these shores.

Toward the end of the 1800s Wedgwood began an entirely new era in pictorial souvenirs through its association with Jones, McDuffee & Stratton. More than 1,100 different views of this nation were produced for the "Sole Import" of that Boston-based firm. These wares were known as "Wedgwood Old Blue Historical," but over the years the line expanded to include more colors than blue and shapes other than plates. These pictorial ceramics gave Wedgwood an eminence in the field which continues to this day.

The plate shown in Plate 95 was made in the 1930s but is similar in style to those made a hundred years earlier, both in the view and the border. Whether it be 1830, 1930, or today, Wedgwood items find a ready market. Wedgwood and its family of firms will probably continue to supply views that we will enjoy for many centuries to come.

95. An old-style view and border on a 9½″ plate which at first glance suggests the 1830s. But it was done in the 1930s by Wedgwood for importation by Jones, McDuffee & Stratton. It shows Park Row and City Hall, New York. *Courtesy of Wedgwood.*

Wood & Sons, Ltd., Burslem

The Wood name is another one of those family names that haxe existed for generations in the potting industry. A previous firm named Enoch Wood & Sons produced some of the most brilliant American views on Staffordshire in the last century. Although the current firm traces its business life back only to 1865, it picked up one of the earlier Wood transfer borders, as shown on the example in Plate 96. This is called the "Grape Vine" and was used on a series of British views more than 150 years ago. The illustrated plate carries the Jones, McDuffee & Stratton seal (the American importer used other firms besides Wedgwood), and the mark on the plate, according to Godden, is one used by Wood from 1931.

96. "The First Church of Christ, Bradford, Mass." This 10″ blue transfer plate was made by Wood in the 1930s, but the border was originally used by Enoch Wood in the 1820s. It also shows "Sole Importer, Jones, McDuffee & Stratton Co."

Royal Century, Warwick

The jug (Plate 87) which bears this name represents somewhat of a mystery in the British pictorial souvenir field. Its marking (shown on page 94) is not listed, nor is the name shown in Godden's *Encyclopedia of British Pottery and Porcelain Marks.* Thus for the moment it is an unknown firm, and an unusual one, for the jug illustrated is of porcelain, whereas most British wares were earthenware. The view of "Trefry House, Digby, N.S." suggests the early part of this century. It carries "England," indicating that it was produced after 1891 and for export, although articles meant for the Canadian market were not required to show country of origin. It is hoped that someone will be able to answer the riddle posed by this souvenir.

GERMAN MANUFACTURERS

Up until the 1930s sizable quantities of ceramic pictorial souvenirs were produced in Germany for the North American market. While German production of souvenirs for the British market ceased with the beginning of World War I, production for these shores continued until the twin effects of depression and war preparations eroded the market and production facilities during the 1930s. The ceramic souvenir trade was never re-established, so if you have an article marked "Made in Germany," you can be sure it was produced no later than the 1930s.

Two world wars have changed much of the map of Europe. The term "German" potting industry, as used here, covers manufacturing in what is today West Germany, East Germany, Poland, Czechoslovakia, and Austria. Unlike Britain's mass concentration of the china industry in one small region, the German industry is scattered over a wide area.

Germany has a long history of ceramic manufacturing, going back to the introduction of porcelain making to Europe at Meissen at the beginning of the 1700s. During that century Meissen and the Royal Berlin Company, founded by King Frederick the Great of Prussia, produced some of the finest porcelain and ornamental wares ever made. By the end of the nineteenth century Germany had a large china manufacturing industry which, like England, was continually looking for new outlets and markets for its production.

The German wares provide the best source of a still completely overlooked aspect of collecting pictorial souvenirs: the shape and style of the ceramic ware itself. Granted the picture has interest and appeal, the surface on which it is found also reflects the culture and taste of the time.

Souvenirs were produced in German factories in immense quantities, in innumerable shapes and design variations. The wares were generally made of porcelain rather than the earthenware favored by the British. They were generally hand-tinted, and frequently the body of the article would have shadings of color to it, again in contrast to the British wares, which were generally transfer-printed in one color. The wares were of good quality, so that today most German articles are found without cracks or chips, although the picture itself may show wear or dullness.

Then, as now, souvenirs had to be inexpensive to appeal to the souvenir instinct and impulse buyer. Maybe the eye was caught by a pierced-border plate with a scene on it. Pierced borders were not produced by the British, but were typical of German pictorial souvenir ware and came in many different variations. Three samples are shown in Plate 97. The plate pierced all the way around was also known as a ribbon plate. With its ribbon threaded through, such plates graced the walls of many a Victorian home.

Thanks to records preserved by John H. Roth & Co., we can get an idea of the wholesale prices of German souvenirs during the 1920s. A sales book shows:

Creamer	2¼ × 3 inch	$2.20 a dozen
Plates	5¼ inch dia.	2.20 " "
Toothpick holder	2 inch high	2.00 " "
Coupe Plates:	8 inch dia.	
Large view, lace border		8.75 " "
Panel views, rococo design		9.00 " "

These prices show a wholesale cost of less than twenty cents for the smaller items and about seventy-five cents for the larger coupe plates. Although more expensive than the 1905 price of ten cents a plate mentioned in Wheelock's ad, they are certainly still at a level almost any traveler could afford.

The number of German factories which produced souvenir wares for the North American market is unknown. American jobbers who ordered the wares made a habit of marking items with their names, as well as the name of the local merchant who ordered the articles

97. Three different examples of German pierced-border plates. L: 4″ double openwork border, "Ocean Pier & Fun Chase, Wildwood, N.J."; C: 6″ "Fayette County Court House, Lexington, Ky." Marked Dresden. Wheelock. Made for the Arcade, Lexington, Kentucky; R: 5″ "Lee-Huckins Hotel and Annex, Oklahoma City, Okla." Wheelock. Made in Germany for Myser China & Glass Co.

produced. But the name of the German manufacturer is seldom included. Some clue can be caught from the habit of adding the region where the item was produced. For example, the articles in the previous illustration were all made for Wheelock, and while two show only "Made in Germany," the plate of the Court House shows "Dresden."

John H. Roth & Co. did not mark its pictorial souvenirs with the name of the German potter, but thanks to correspondence in the 1950s with its previous German agent, we learned the names of some of the potters it used. This correspondence shows that the manufacturers for Roth were located in Thuringia, now a part of East Germany. At least some of the potters who made souvenirs for Roth between 1910 and the 1930s were: Adolf Harrass Nachfolger, Grossbreitenbach; M. Freitag, Grossbreitenbach; Bauer & Lehmann of Kahla.

In some cases American importers not only had wares made to order by German potters but owned or had an ownership interest in the factories. Several major American import firms during the period 1890–1915 advertised their own manufacturing plants and the range of wares that they were able to produce. Most of this manufacturing effort was certainly directed to the wider tableware and ornament porcelain trade, but some of the import–owners seemed to have also had an interest in the ceramic pictorial souvenir field. Several of the items shown carry the marks of firms that were controlled or closely associated with American importers.

J. P. Cushion's *Pocket Book of German Ceramic Marks* (London: Faber & Faber, Ltd., 1961) has been used as the major source of potters' names, locations, and dates. Information on the American importers has been developed primarily from a review of old issues of the *Crockery and Glass Journal*. However, there are still unknown marks, and some are shown here.

In the listing that follows, marked wares are identified and described where they have been found. Certainly this listing is not complete. In time other firms and marks will undoubtedly come to light.

L. S. & S., CARLSBAD

This mark is illustrated at the end of this section and is found on the plate shown in Plate 98 of New York's City Hall. That building had been pictured on Staffordshire in the 1820s, but this scene certainly suggests the end of the 1800s, or perhaps the beginning of this century. The mark is identified from information in the *Crockery and Glass Journal* as being the initials of L. Straus & Sons, a New York-based importing firm that dates back to 1866. The firm owned or controlled facilities in Europe to produce many kinds of ceramic articles. One of the Straus sons broke away to co-found the department store of Abraham & Straus, still well-known to New Yorkers today.

98. City Hall, New York on an 8¼″ porcelain plate dating to about the beginning of the century. Made for L. Straus & Sons.

99. Two pictorial souvenirs made for B. F. H. S. China (Benj. F. Hunt & Sons) of Haida, Austria, and Boston, Massachusetts: L to R: 3″ yellow background sugar bowl with scene of "High School Building, Laconia, N.H."; 7″ hand-painted plate with view showing "Evangelical Church, Westboro, Mass."

B.F.H.S., AUSTRIA

An advertisement in the Christmas issue of the 1895 *Crockery and Glass Journal* shows this mark found on the two articles shown in Plate 99, and the information that Benj. F. Hunt & Sons have their own firm at Haida, Carlsbad, Austria, and can provide a total range of inexpensive porcelain wares. The firm was an American importer with an address at 53 Hanover Street, Boston, Massachusetts.

VICTORIA, CARLSBAD

Porcelain was made at Alt-Rohlau in Carlsbad at a factory named the Porzellanfabrik Viktoria. It was established by Schmidt & Co. in 1883 and produced a wide range of porcelain wares destined for export. The firm was linked to Lazarus & Rosenfeld, a New York importer, but whether it was an importer only or a part owner is now not clear. The Victoria mark was also used on pictorial souvenirs marketed in England as described by Ian Henderson in *Pictorial Souvenirs of Britain*.

Wares from this factory in Carlsbad reflect the unsettled history of central Europe. Ian Henderson mentions that wares marked Carlsbad would have been stamped Bohemia before 1891. Afterward they would have been labeled Austria (as does the item illustrated in Plate 100) until 1918 when Czechoslovakia would have appeared on articles produced for export.

CARL SCHUMANN, ARZBERG, BAVARIA

Schumann was a profuse producer of ribbon plates and a wide range of other souvenir wares for both the British and American markets. The firm was founded in 1871 and manufactured and decorated all types of porcelain for export. The illustration in Plate 101 is of a shallow pierced-border bowl.

PORZELLANFABRIK TETTAU, TETTAU, FRANCONIA

This very old porcelain factory traces its origin back to 1794. It takes its name from its location in Tettau, which is further represented by the letter "T" found on the shield of the trademark. As with other makers mentioned, this firm produced pictorial souvenirs for both the English and American markets. An example is the jug in Plate 101.

100. Small cobalt blue cup and saucer. Made by Victoria. Cup: "Liberty Bell, Old State House, Philadelphia, Pa." Saucer: "Girard College, Philadelphia, Pa."

101. "View of Peachblossom Creek, near Easton, Md." 6½″ curved openwork border bowl. Schumann of Arzberg. "Nichols Memorial Library" of Kingston, Massachusetts on a 3¼″ jug made by Tettau.

SCHLESISCHE PORZELLANFABRIK, TIEFENFURT, SILESIA

This firm was established in 1883 as a subsidiary of P. Donath (which dates back to 1808), and the example shown in Plate 102 is marked with crossed swords and the letter "S." Perhaps this was an attempt to imitate the Meissen mark, or at least cause confusion to prospective purchasers. It may be that this firm limited itself to souvenir-style wares while the older parent firm produced a broad range of tableware and other items for export.

SCHWARZENHAMMER, BAVARIA

The Niagara Falls souvenir shown in Plate 103 carries a mark on it which appears at the end of this section. But the mark is not found in Cushion, although Schwarzenhammer is a town in which there was a firm by the name of Schumann & Schreider. However, that firm, according to Cushion, used other marks on its wares.

RUDOLSTADT, THURINGIA

Another firm associated with L. Straus & Sons was located in Rudolstadt, and according to an advertisement in the Christmas 1906 issue of the *Crockery and Glass Journal*, "The New York and Rudolstadt Pottery Co. [was] pre-eminent as makers of bric-a-brac among factories of the world." The advertisement shows the R.W. trademark found on the pair of mugs shown in Plate 104. The mark is given on page 93.

C. & E. CARSTENS, BLANKENHAIN, THURINGIA

A mark combining a shield and the word "Weimar" was used as one of the trademarks of C. & E. Carstens, which produced porcelain in Blankenhain, Thuringia, during the first quarter of this century. The small dish of "Holiday House, Milford, N.H." (Plate 105) bears this firm's mark and the information that it was made for Emerson & Son of Milford, New Hampshire.

LORENZ HUTSCHENREUTHER, SELB, BAVARIA

This factory, established in 1856, produced porcelain at Selb, Bavaria, and is known to have engaged in export trade. The plate shown, of good-quality porcelain, bears the firm's mark, showing it was manufactured in Germany, but it includes a second mark indicating that the decoration was added by the American firm of Tatler & Lawson of Trenton, New Jersey. The plate in Plate 106 has heavy gold border decoration.

102. "The Dumplings, Jamestown, R.I." Small 3¾″ dish. Schlesische Porzellanfabrik.

103. View of Niagara Falls on 3¼″ heart-shaped openwork basket. Schwarzenhammer.

104. Two mugs produced by Rudolstadt with views of Bay City, Michigan: L to R: "Hotel Wenona and Park, Bay City, Mich."; "Federal Building, Bay City, Mich."

105. L to R: "Holiday House, Milford, N.H." 4½″ brown transfer plate made by C & E Carstens. Weimar mark; "The Public Library Boston" 6½″ dish with the unidentified Elbogen mark.

106. "The Capitol." 9¾" heavy gold-edged porcelain plate with hand-painted view. Plate was made by Hutschenreuther and decorated by the Trenton, New Jersey, firm of Tatler & Lawson.

Other Makers and Marks
Several other marks have been observed, but to date we have not been able to identify them from information in Cushion or other sources. In some cases the town will be shown as having a porcelain manufacturer, but not one which reflects the mark found on these examples. In any event, these items must be unattributed as to manufacturer, and in a few cases as to location where they were made.

Altenburg, Thuringia
Although porcelain manufacturers are shown for this town, none has been found with the mark shown on page 94 and found on the illustrated jug in Plate 107, showing "U.S. Life Saving Station, Salisbury Beach, Mass."

107. "U.S. Life Savings Station, Salisbury Beach, Mass." 4½″ hand-colored jug made in Altenburg, Thuringia, for M. H. Farrell of Salisbury Beach, Mass.

108. "The Soldiers National Cemetery, Gettysburg, Pa." 7½″ yellow border plate with the unidentified mark G. H. S. Co.

ARZBERG, BAVARIA

The firm of Carl Schumann has already been mentioned as manufacturing in this town. But the mark found on the vase with Niagara Falls (Plate 109) does not match that of any known company located here.

ELBOGEN, AUSTRIA

Three potters operated here, according to Cushion, and all of them made porcelain during the first part of this century. They were: Spring & Co., c. 1900; Heinrich Kretschmann, c. 1900; Adolf Persch, c. 1902. None of those makers' marks is similar to the one found on the shallow dish with a view of "The Public Library Boston" (Plate 105) and bearing the mark depicted on page 94.

G. H. S., Co., BAVARIA

Gettysburg is the subject of a plate with the mark given on page 93, which also cannot be identified.

109. Two more views of Niagara Falls by two unidentified makers: 5½"
basket shows C/N mark, Bavaria; 6½" vase with P/A mark, Arzberg,
Bavaria.

C. & N., BAVARIA

The basket is another ceramic shape used for pictorial souvenirs; the
one shown in Plate 109 bears a very familiar view. The mark appears
on page 93, and it is unattributed as to the maker.

M. W. Co., GERMANY

This mark, shown on page 93, is on the jug depicting a church in
Dark Harbor, Maine (see Plate 68). It is not found in references, and
the maker must at the moment be considered unknown.

AMERICAN MANUFACTURERS AND DECORATORS

The American potting industry, by comparison to that of England and
Europe, is a recent development. Through much of the nineteenth
century all tableware and other ceramics, to say nothing of pictorial
souvenirs, were made overseas and imported.

But in this century the story has changed to some degree. To begin
with, premiums and advertising or promotional items were produced
domestically. Then some pictorial souvenirs for major tourist attractions were done here. Later, ceramic wares in limited editions tended
to originate in this country. If a church is having a celebration and feels
it can sell 1,000 plates, or a club is having its centennial and wants a tile
produced, these today may be produced in the United States. The

quantity is small, and generally the lead time between desire and delivery is not very long.

Frequently today, in the domestic production of souvenirs, two different types of firms are involved. One is the potting manufacturer which may sell its wares in the blank (i.e., plain, undecorated). The other is the decorator or small art studio which adds the scene or art work desired by the client, and which may refire the ware to preserve the decoration.

Relatively new is the pictorial souvenir designed to appeal to a large geographic area. Items are produced today for an entire region or state. They can then be marketed to any merchant in the area. These newer items lack the personal touch of turn-of-the-century items that were produced for a specific merchant, but they can be produced and stocked in larger quantities.

The following listing describes a few of the major domestic firms that have engaged in the pictorial souvenir field, and a few of the major decorator firms. This list is again not complete, but merely a sample of domestic producers of pictorial ceramics.

MAKERS

BUFFALO POTTERY, BUFFALO, NEW YORK

Probably the best-known American manufacturer of ceramics is the Buffalo Pottery, which has made several distinct styles and bodies of wares that have all found favor with collectors. The firm was founded in 1901 when the Larkin Soap Co. established facilities to produce premiums for customers who purchased its soap products. Buffalo Pottery initially devoted all its production to the parent company, but in time expanded to sell other items through regular distribution channels. Our interest is limited to a rather small number of pieces which were offered as premiums and had pictorial views produced on plates or jugs.

The items of interest as pictorial souvenirs were premiums offered beginning in 1905 when a series of six historical scenes were shown in the premium catalogue. These were 10″ plates available in either a pale green or pale blue transfer, and the views offered were: The Capitol, the White House, Mount Vernon, Niagara Falls, Faneuil Hall, and Independence Hall (Plate 58). Later other series were added in color, and other items were produced as advertising or promotional wares for firms besides the Larkin company. The item illustrated in Plates 110 and 111 is one of five historical views done on jugs. This view, "The Whaling City. Souvenir of New Bedford, Mass.," was first shown in the 1907 catalogue. Since the 1920s, Buffalo Pottery has produced institutional and hotel ware only.

110 and 111. "The Whaling City. Souvenir of New Bedford, Mass." is on the spout of this 6″ underglazed green jug with views on both sides. Buffalo Pottery, Buffalo, New York.

LAMBERTON/SCAMMELL, TRENTON, NEW JERSEY

Lamberton is the name of a pottery which dates back to 1893 when it was owned and operated by Thomas Maddock, an Englishman who had potted in this country since the Civil War. Later D. William Scammell took over the works and produced two grades of dinnerware marked "Trenton China" and "Lamberton China."

The plate illustrated in Plate 112 was produced in 1941 when it was advertised as being one of "The first set of Historical American Views on China made in the USA." There were twelve different views produced on bone china plates from engravings by a Mr. DeKoort to commemorate the 200th year of the founding of Bethlehem, Pennsylvania. The plates were made for the "Busy Workers" of the Moravian Church and sold originally for $20 a dozen.

HOMER LAUGHLIN CHINA CO., NEWELL, WEST VIRGINIA

In 1873 Homer and his brother Shakespeare Laughlin started a pottery in East Liverpool, Ohio, which became the first devoted exclusively to white ware. Later the firm moved across the river to Newell, West Virginia, where "the largest plant in the world" was opened in 1906. Homer Laughlin stated in his advertisements that he was "producing the largest output of any pottery firm in America or England." Whether these claims were gospel or puffery, Homer Laughlin was without question a well-known firm which produced a wide variety of ceramics for the American market, including the pictorial souvenir of the White House which is shown in Plate 113.

112. Interior of the Moravian Church, Bethlehem, Pennsylvania, on a 10¾" pink porcelain plate. Behind the picture of each of the four individuals who were associated with the early church and Bethlehem is their name in their own handwriting. Lamberton/Scamell, Trenton, New Jersey.

113. L to R: "The White House" on a 7" plate with State seals around the border. Homer Laughlin China Co., Newell, West Virginia; "New York Chamber of Commerce" on a 6½" plate made by Pope-Gosser China, Coshocton, Ohio.

POPE GOSSER CHINA, COSHOCTON, OHIO

This firm used as its motto "The Pottery where Quality Counts" and primarily produced dinner services. But it also engaged to some degree in the souvenir or commemorative field, as shown by this plate of the New York Chamber of Commerce, illustrated in Plate 113. The plate may have been a giveaway offered to merchants of New York sometime after the building was opened in 1901. Today the building is still in use, but the ground floor is now a department store, while the Chamber of Commerce holds forth in the upper chambers.

SHENANGO POTTERY CO., NEW CASTLE, PENNSYLVANIA

This firm is known for its table and hotel wares, but produced what could be called pictorial souvenirs in dinnerware for the Baltimore & Ohio Railroad's dining cars (see Plate 45). That particular series was most popular, and it had been produced by both Buffalo Pottery and Lamberton China.

DECORATORS

WORLD WIDE ART STUDIOS, COVINGTON, TENNESSEE

Mr. W. M. Snyder, the president of this firm, states, "I think it would be impossible to guess how many millions of Commemorative Plates we have made for organizations throughout the United States since starting in the early 1940s." Two are shown in Plate 114. The firm limits itself to plates or tiles, but provides a prospective client a variety of different styles and colors from which to choose. The decorators work from a photograph or from an architect's or artist's drawing. Up to 100 words of copy, telling the history of the organization or the scene depicted, is fired onto the back of the article.

DELANO STUDIOS, SETAUKET, NEW YORK

This firm began in 1946 "with a process of ceramic decoration developed to utilize the best features of hand painting and printing." Commemorative wares are only one part of their business, and they feature "hand-colored" scenes on a variety of ceramic, glass, and enameled surfaces. They will add copy to the back, but are much more concerned in the production of a quality picture on the facing surface. Two samples of its wares are shown in Plate 115.

VERNON KILNS, LOS ANGELES, CALIFORNIA

This firm produced plates of a distinctive nature. They are heavy, transfer-printed, generally multi-view, and once you have seen one, others are easy to identify as coming from the same firm. Many cover an entire state or region, as do these examples in Plate 116.

114. Plates produced by World Wide Art Studios of Covington, Tennessee: "Masonic Temple, Springfield, Col.," 8¼" plate; "The Reformed Church of Oradell, Oradell, N.J.," 9½" plate.

115. Hand-painted wares by Delano Studios: "The Three Village Inn, Stony Brook, N.Y.," 6" tile; "Woodland Ferry, Del.," 10" plate.

116. A pair of 10½" plates decorated by Vernon Kilns, Los Angeles. L to R: six views of San Bernardino, California, in blue transfer; multi-views of Oklahoma on a pink transfer plate.

TATLER & LAWSON, TRENTON, NEW JERSEY

Where a "blank" was made by a firm other than the one that did the decoration, the maker generally is not shown, and the blank may actually have been a "second"—that is, a piece of imperfect quality.

An exception is the good-quality porcelain plate (Plate 106) which carries the mark of Lorenz Hutschenreuther as well as that of Tatler & Lawson. It is probable that the rich gold gilt border was added by this American firm, and perhaps the center view also.

Tatler Decorating Company dates back to the nineteenth century when it was named for its founder, William H. Tatler. In this century Lawrence P. Lawson joined the firm and added his name.

JAPANESE MANUFACTURERS

Japan has exported many varieties of inexpensive ceramic novelties throughout much of this century. However, not until the 1950s did she enter the pictorial souvenir field in force. Once again it was up to American distributors to place the orders with the Japanese firms.

The wares do not bear the mark of the manufacturer, but rather the phrase "Made in Japan." Sometimes this will be on a small sticker that can be pulled off or may wear off. Other markings may include a stamp of the importer, such as is shown on these wares (Plates 117 and 118) made for ENCO National Co. This is probably the major firm engaged in all aspects of the souvenir field today. It has been in business since 1909 both as manufacturer and distributor, and George Duclos, its president, states that he personally designed the spoon rest form shown here.

The examples illustrate the two major processes used for ceramic pictorials today: hand painting or a transfer decal. Currently the wares from Japan command the lowest prices, perhaps because they are so new. For another example of Japanese ceramic wares see Plate 149.

MARKS

The marks shown are those found on the articles illustrated. Only trademarks or distinctive methods of showing a name have been included. If the identification is simply the name of the firm, it has not been reproduced here. Nor do we suggest that the marks shown are the only ones used by that particular firm, for many potters frequently changed the manner of signing their wares.

117. "Glacier National Park." 6″ openwork hand-painted plate. Made in Japan for ENCO, New York.

118. "Souvenir of Ocean City, N.J." Spoon rest in the shape of a coffeepot. Made in Japan for ENCO, New York.

British Potters' Marks:
(1) William Adams & Sons; (2) British Anchor Pottery Co., Ltd.; (3) Alma Ware (Thomas Cone, Ltd.); (4) Crown Ducal (A. G. Richardson & Co., Ltd.); (5) Royal Doulton; (6) Foley China (Wileman & Co.); (7) William Henry Goss, Ltd.; (8) Mason's; (9) Mintons; (10) Ridgways; (11) Royal Winton (Grimwades, Ltd.); (12) Spode, Ltd.; (13) Tuscan China (R H & S L Plant, Ltd.); (14) Wood & Sons, Ltd.

German Manufacturers' Marks:
(1) L. Straus & Sons, Manufacturer and New York Importer; (2) Victoria (Schmidt & Co.), Carlsbad, Austria; (3) Carl Schumann, Arzberg, Bavaria; (4) Porzellanfabrik Tettau, Tettau, Franconia; (5) Schlesische Porzellan-fabrik, Tiefenfurt; (6) Schwarzenhammer, Bavaria; (7) Unidentified; (8) Unidentified; (9) Unidentified; (10) Millstone mark found on many articles (sometimes the manufacturer, importer, or local merchant will also be shown); (11) Rudolstadt, Thuringia, a firm associated with L. Straus & Sons; (12) Unidentified; ENCO National Co., a New York importer which has many items produced in Japan.

1.

ALTENBURG

China
Made in Germany

2.

MADE IN AUSTRIA

3.

BAVARIA

4.

5.

ROYAL
CENTURY

ENGLAND

6.

7.

Miscellaneous Manufacturers' Marks:
(1) Weimar (C & E Carstens), Thuringia; (2) Unidentified, German; (3) Unidentified, German; (4) Lorenz Hutschenreuther, Selb, Bavaria; (5) Tatler & Lawson, Trenton, New Jersey; (6) Unidentified, England; (7) Bridgewood & Son, England.

American Marks:

Distributors: (1) The Wheelock trademark combining the wheel with the cross-bar of a lock; (2) Another Wheelock mark which included the name of the merchant for whom the wares had been produced; (3) A JON-ROTH German mark (the company also employed a mark similar to (2), with either JONROTH or John H. Roth & Co., and information concerning the merchant for whom the wares were made); JONROTH British trademark (sometimes the wares also carried the phrase "Old English Staffordshire Ware"); (5) Jones, McDuffee & Stratton Co., Boston-based importer long associated with Wedgwood; (6) Rowland & Marsellus, a New York importer of ceramics.

Potters: (7) Buffalo Pottery, Buffalo, New York; (8) Lamberton-Scammell, Trenton, New Jersey; (9) Shenango, New Castle, Pennsylvania.

Decorators: (10) World Wide Art Studios, Covington, Tennessee; (11) Delano Studios, Setauket, New York.

Part II

*World's Fairs
& Expositions*

Any coverage of world's fairs would be incomplete without mention of "The Great Exhibition of the Works of Industry of All Nations" held in London in 1851. No one called it by its official name, and it has always been known by the name of the magnificent building in which it was housed: The Crystal Palace.

The building was designed by Joseph Paxton, a gardener turned engineer, who got his inspiration for the design from a water lily leaf. The support of the building resembled the long spine of the water lily stem with the leaf itself made of glass. Stipulations imposed by the sponsors of the British exhibition were that the structure destroy as little as possible of Hyde Park, so the building was built on top of the ground, and even incorporated clumps of existing trees within the building. It was the first modular building, being prefabbed in sections of 24 feet, which facilitated another requirement: that the building be removed at the end of the exhibition. Although people at first were afraid that the structure might blow away or crash down, the public quickly became enthusiastic over the design and crowds gathered to watch its construction. Originally it had been hoped that the building would be 1,851 feet long—one foot for each year—but because of the modular design, the length came out to 1,848 feet. It was 450 feet wide and had the effect of a huge botanical enclosure.

The Crystal Palace was officially opened by Queen Victoria on May 1, 1851, and housed a great collection of works of industry and the arts from all over the world. The exhibition ran for almost six months, attracted close to six million visitors, and set a high standard of excellence. It also paid a profit to its backers; few of its successors have been as fortunate.

The first world's fair in this country was a faded imitation of the London success. Just two years after the opening of the exhibition in London, a Crystal Palace was built in New York City in Bryant Park at 42nd Street and was opened on July 14, 1853. It was planned as an exhibition celebrating the industry of all nations and to show Americans what they had not been able to see in London. The concept was bold, but it got a bad press, as we would say today, and was considered hostile to American industry. In addition, the building was poorly put together and leaked water onto the exhibits and the visitors. One story says that contracts for construction were let three times—each time with different specifications. If so, some of the difficulties are understandable.

The New York Crystal Palace was not successful, and the building was destroyed by fire four years later.

CENTENNIAL EXPOSITION, PHILADELPHIA, 1876

Four years of planning and almost two years of actual building went into the Centennial Exposition held in Philadelphia in 1876. It billed itself as the largest exhibition ever held: in both space under roof— 60 acres of exhibit area—and grounds—256 acres of wooded and open spaces in Fairmount Park along the Schuylkill River. The exhibition was housed in 5 major exposition buildings and some 150 additional buildings sponsored by organizations, states, and 35 foreign countries.

Opening day was May 10, 1876. The night was wet and the forecast for the day unsettled. But Philadelphia was nonetheless literally enveloped in bunting, and every flagpole and halyard had a flag flying from it. At sunrise the bell in Independence Hall started to peal. By 7 A.M. there was a mass of people at the gates. At nine when the gates opened a continuous river of people poured into the Exposition grounds. But the outpouring was of people, not the skies. By mid-morning the drizzle stopped, the clouds broke, and the sun shone forth dazzlingly.

A contingent of the National Guard of Pennsylvania preceded the large official party. As each of the major foreign guests entered, they were met with the strains of their own country's national anthem. After

President Grant and his wife had entered and all were in place, the Centennial Grand March, composed by Richard Wagner for the event, was played. There followed prayers for the Exposition and the nation, and an address by President Grant, which ended precisely at noon, when, at a signal, the American flag was run up to the highest point of the main exposition building, and the Centennial was officially declared open.

Some of the inventions that the fairgoer could examine among the 30,000 exhibits were "the little wonder"—a sewing machine by Singer; a wallpaper printing press; an ice crusher; the talking instrument of Alexander Graham Bell; the typewriter, and the telegraph of Thomas Alva Edison. Or if he was hungry, he might sample the wares of S. F. Whitman & Son, Confectionary, which demonstrated how candy was made.

One of the more unusual exhibits was that of the hand holding the torch of the Statue of Liberty. The statue and site in New York harbor were not to be completed for another decade. Today few people remember that at least a part of The Lady spent her early days in the United States in Philadelphia.

For the daring there was Sawyer's Observatory, towering 185 feet into the sky from a height of land already 410 feet above the Schuylkill River. It was composed of a main shaft around which was built a doughnut-type cage, large enough to accommodate forty people, which "worked on the principle of the elevator, so recently introduced in our lofty buildings." At the top of the ascent was a twenty-foot platform, surrounded by a railing and wire net to prevent accidents. The viewer was permitted up to ten minutes to see the Exposition and all of Philadelphia spread out below. Besides this, the Centennial had no amusement section, as later fairs would feature.

Souvenirs of the fair could be obtained at the exhibit of Gillinder & Sons, glassmakers, which demonstrated how to make glass. Other items were available for those who actually visited the Centennial, but many additional items were produced and sold throughout the United States in honor of the event. You did not have to go to the exhibition to obtain some souvenir of it.

Today most souvenirs of the Centennial in Philadelphia are no longer inexpensive. They are sought after, and many command a high price. The souvenirs shown in Plates 119 and 120 are typical of the kind of thing made for the exhibition. The glass bread platter has been produced in a similar style for the 200th anniversary. If your dollars are limited, you might do better to collect bicentennial souvenirs.

The Centennial Exposition of 1876 ran for 159 days and attracted some eight million visitors. It also was profitable and repaid its backers.

119. A 7½″ high Wedgwood pitcher created for the Centennial in Philadelphia in 1876. The names of the thirteen original States encircle the collar. (*All articles shown in this Chapter are courtesy of Larry Zimmerman and were photographed by him from his personal collection.*)

JULY 4TH 1876

120. A glass bread plate produced for the Centennial, showing the signers of the Declaration of Independence. 13½″ x 9½″. (A similar plate has been produced for the Bicentennial showing "200 Years Ago.")

WORLD'S COLUMBIAN EXPOSITION, CHICAGO, 1893

The World's Columbian Exposition was held to celebrate the 400th anniversary of the discovery of America by Columbus. True, 1492 plus 400 doesn't equal 1893, but the planning and construction were a little slow. Most people would agree the extra year was worth the wait, for it was a magnificent affair.

The exposition was held on the banks of Lake Michigan on some 650 acres of wasteland and land-fill planned and landscaped by Frederick Law Olmsted, the designer of New York's Central Park, to suggest a Midwest Venice with a system of lagoons passing every major building. The main buildings had steel framework to permit large expanses of interior space, but the exteriors were uniformly classical in style. The exposition gained the title "The White City" from the way the buildings shone like marble during the day and were reflected day and night in the lagoons. The night reflections came from a new invention introduced at the fair and used to outline the major buildings: the electric light.

The theme of the fair was symbolized in two statues which faced each other at opposite ends of the Court of Honor: Columbus seated in a stone boat rowed by buxom females manning large stone oars at one end, and the Statue of the Republic standing with her outstretched upright arms at the opposite end, ready to receive Columbus and the generations of men who would follow him.

The story of the exposition was industry and invention, as suggested by the Machinery Building shown on the Wedgwood plate in Plate 121. Another invention was introduced here which is only now coming into more common use—the moving sidewalk. The Casino Pier had a moving sidewalk of 4,300 feet to bring steamboat passengers ashore. It consisted of two parallel belts, one moving at three miles an hour and the other at twice that speed. You stepped onto the first, and then from that to the faster one. The cost of the walk was five cents.

Although the moving sidewalk had been introduced with a utilitarian purpose, another invention first introduced at the exposition was only for fun. That was the Ferris Wheel, named for the man who designed it. It stood 264 feet high in the Midway amusement section of the fair and had 36 passenger coaches, each of which accommodated 60 people. Fully loaded, the wheel could lift 2,160 people aloft. It was higher than any building in Chicago at that time, and a ride cost fifty cents.

Women had their own building at this exposition, as they had had at the Centennial Exposition. A competition had been sponsored among female architects, and fourteen women, all under twenty-five years of age, submitted designs. The winning plan, by Sophia Hayden of Boston, was an Italian Renaissance building featuring a roof garden with palms and fountains. Souvenirs were sold there, and two of the most popular were a metal replica of the Woman's Building, and a souvenir spoon also showing the building. This fair was a major impetus to the souvenir spoon craze (see Plate 146 for an illustration of the official spoon of the exposition).

121. Pictorial souvenirs from the World's Columbia Exposition, Chicago, 1893. The Wedgwood plate is one of a sereis of six with views of the major buildings. This 8½″ plate is in blue, although shades of brown, red, and black transfer were also made. The bone dish is by Bridgwood & Son and shows "Lagoon Looking South"; the glass salt and pepper show the Government Building and another view of the Machinery Building.

PAN AMERICAN EXPOSITION, BUFFALO, NEW YORK, 1901

This exposition differed from its American predecessors in that it did not commemorate an historical event. The purpose of this fair was to promote social and commercial interests among the countries of the Western Hemisphere. The symbol of the fair was a 375-foot-high tower topped by a Goddess of Light as shown on the glass souvenir plate in Plate 122. Electricity was still a relatively new invention. The tower was lit by electricity generated from the waters of Niagara Falls. Among the inventions introduced at the fair were Edison's wireless telegraph and his storage battery.

Watch fobs, stickpins, souvenir spoons, tokens, medals, and the items shown in Plate 122 were among the souvenirs produced for this exposition. But the Pan American's major claim to fame was a tragedy. It was at a reception being held in the exposition's Temple of Music in September 1901 that President McKinley was assassinated.

122. Samples of souvenirs from the Pan-American Exposition, Buffalo, 1901: L: Metal Buffalo, 3″ high, 3½″ long; C: Glass 7½″ ribbon plate with view of "Electric Tower"; R: Jar with metal relief work, 3½″ top.

LOUISIANA PURCHASE EXPOSITION, ST. LOUIS, MISSOURI, 1904

"Meet Me in St. Louis, Louis, Meet Me at the Fair" . . . that is the song that has immortalized this event for many Americans. The reason for the Universal Exposition, which was the official name of the event, was to celebrate the 100th anniversary of the Louisiana Purchase. But as with the earlier exposition in Chicago, ideas ran ahead of construction and the fair was not held until the 101st anniversary of the purchase. The exposition committee budgeted for the exposition the same amount that had been paid for the entire Louisiana Purchase a century before— 15 million dollars. For that the committee got an impressive array of white marble-like buildings plus waterfalls, cascades, statues, and bridges to tie the elegant scene together. All were lit at night, including the cascades of water.

The theme of this fair was the application of science to everyday life. We may smile at some of the exhibits, but the theme was appropriately carried out. One exhibit showed cooking being done by electricity! Another had 100 motor cars on display, along with the contraption Orville and Wilbur Wright had successfully flown the year before— the airplane. Two other items were introduced at the fair, without which summer would be unbearable today: the ice-cream cone and iced tea. The most shocking thing about the iced tea was that it was introduced by a Britisher. He found he could not sell his hot tea in the hot Missouri summer, so he decided to cool it with ice, and it became the hit drink of the fair. But his own nation has never to this day added iced tea to its summer menus.

The exposition had an amusement section called the Pike where one could find souvenirs and fun along with food and pleasure. Ruby glass souvenirs were probably the major new souvenir item introduced at the fair. Some of them are shown in Plate 138. Other souvenirs revealed a French influence, as seen in the plate illustrated (see Plate 123) among the sample of wares from this fair.

PANAMA-PACIFIC EXPOSITION, SAN FRANCISCO, CALIFORNIA, 1915
PANAMA-CALIFORNIA EXPOSITION, SAN DIEGO, CALIFORNIA, 1915–1916

These two fairs were in celebration of a contemporary event: the completion of the Panama Canal. The San Francisco fair was international in scope and ran from February to December 1915; the San Diego fair

123. The French influence of the St. Louis Exposition as shown on a French-made 8¼″ porcelain plate. The 4¾″ high tumbler is marked "Victoria/Carlsbad/Austria"; the pink demi-tasse cup and saucer of the "Palace of Electricity" is unmarked, although probably German; a small hand souvenir mirror depicts "Festival Hall."

124. Some of the 120,000 jewels from the Pan-Pacific Exposition of San Francisco in 1915. These were sold as souvenirs. The Heinz pickles were probably promotional giveaways, and the 10″ rolled-edge blue-and-white Rowland & Marsellus plate was "Designed by United Souvenir & Novelty Co., 1150 Market St., San Francisco."

concentrated on California and the Western Hemisphere and ran for two years. Although the reason for the fairs was an extraordinary engineering event, industry and invention were not their themes.

San Francisco highlighted art and beauty. The symbol of the fair was the "Tower of Jewels," a 500-foot tower adorned by more than 120,000 jewels on its seven levels of excess—all of which glistened in the California sun by day and were lit by masked lights and searchlights at night. The jewels were also sold as souvenirs, and it can be hoped that the ones in the accompanying illustration (Plate 124) were obtained by purchase rather than by souvenir hunters. The tower provided a nightly equivalent of a major Hollywood opening of a later date. The extensive use of electric lights in all styles and colors gained the fair its nickname: The Light Fair.

The fair was held in Presidio Park in San Francisco. Its pavilion reflected a blend of Moorish, Spanish, and Mediterranean styles. The fairgoer could walk the grounds, or take the "Overland Fair, Limited" train around the borders, or the "Fadgl Auto Train" along the avenues. Either ride cost a dime. Motion pictures were a new form of entertainment and were also used by exhibitors to transmit information.

One of the commercial pavilions that rivaled the Tower of Jewels was that of the H. Heinz Company. The roof of the building was a pyramid of the firm's products, with each of the 57 varieties allotted one circular tier, all capped by a huge "57."

San Diego's fair ran concurrently with San Francisco's, and then continued for another year at its location in Balboa Park.

SESQUICENTENNIAL EXPOSITION, PHILADELPHIA, 1926

Philadelphia was the home of the celebration of the 150th anniversary of the nation's birth. It was not held in Fairmount Park, the locale of the Centennial Exposition fifty years earlier, but in League Island Park, at the foot of Broad Street, near the Philadelphia Naval Yard. Broad Street was renamed "Avenue of Nations" for the event, and more than 100 acres were converted to exposition space and an amusement area called the Gladway. The fair opened on May 31, 1926, and its stress was on 150 years of "Life, Liberty, Happiness." The symbol of the fair was what by now should have been a somewhat hackneyed idea—a 200-foot Tower of Light. The souvenir shown in Plate 125 suggests the reworking of another symbol, the Liberty Bell. Over all, the fair was low-key and not really successful.

CENTURY OF PROGRESS, CHICAGO 1933–1934

During the middle of the Depression the Chicago Century of Progress was a bright spot in an otherwise clouded economy. It was held on the original site of the 1893 exposition, with the addition of some new land-fill out into Lake Michigan. Its theme was the "Dramatization of the progress of civilization during the 100 years of Chicago's existence." But that was too long a phrase, and it was simply called the Century of Progress, marking the 100th year since Fort Dearborn became Chicago.

The buildings for the most part were prefabricated and featured clean, streamlined shapes that were in sharp contrast to the overdone styles of previous fairs. Industry and invention were the keynotes of

125. Liberty Bell bank. 4″ high heavy metal. Souvenir of the 1926 Sesquicentennial, Philadelphia.

126. A sample of souvenirs showing the Art Deco flavor of the 1933 "Century of Progress," Chicago. The mug has a female body handle and is in green ceramic, 6½″ high. The "key" is a letter opener, and the 2¾″ medal was the official one issued for the fair. The bank was a promotional article of American Can Company. On the left are two decks of cards and their box with themes of the fair.

the fair. Art Deco themes and styles were in evidence in many of the exhibits, and on souvenirs, as shown in the samples illustrated in Plate 126. Air conditioning and neon lighting were new features, and space was sold to exhibitors for the first time. At all previous expositions, space had been given free to would-be exhibitors.

The Century of Progress ran for two years during the summer and fall of 1933 and 1934. It attracted 38 million visitors and was a good business investment for its backers, paying full value on its bonds plus 6 per cent interest. In the middle of the hard-money days of the Depression, that was not bad.

On the last night of the fair, October 30, 1934, some half a million people came to the fair to see the closing ceremony and the fireworks display. It might have been that it was trick-or-treat night, for apparently a strong souvenir instinct took hold of the crowd and the visitors literally started to tear down the buildings. Thus today there may be some unique souvenirs of the Century of Progress in some Chicago homes.

GOLDEN GATE INTERNATIONAL EXPOSITION, SAN FRANCISCO, CALIFORNIA, 1939–1940

Chicago filled in a small part of Lake Michigan to expand the area for their fair in 1933. San Francisco went one better. That city created "the largest artificial island in the world"—400 acres of fill right in the middle of San Francisco Bay. From this created island named Treasure Island you could see the two other celebrated engineering triumphs of the city, the Golden Gate Bridge and the San Francisco–Oakland Bay Bridge. The island had been created with the idea that it would become "an ultra-modern metropolitan airport" after the fair and make San Francisco "America's air crossroads of the Pacific." But those plans changed as World War II came along and the Navy moved to Treasure Island, never to leave.

The architecture was of a style termed "Pacifica," employing motifs from both the eastern and western shores of the Pacific. The symbol of the fair was a 400-foot-high Tower of the Sun, which housed a 40-bell carillon and dominated the island by both sight and sound. Two of the souvenirs shown in Plate 127 might be considered symbolic, for they permitted one to look at oneself and to put on a new face.

There were pavilions and exhibitions from twenty foreign nations, most of them grouped in two areas called "Pacific Basin Area" and "Latin American Court," which suggests the nations and areas represented at the exposition.

The fair opened in February 1939 and ran for two years.

NEW YORK WORLD'S FAIR, 1939–1940

Even with World War II breaking out in Europe, the theme of the 1939 New York World's Fair was "Building the World of Tomorrow." The fair was built on what had been a swamp and garbage dump in Flushing Meadow and featured modern architecture. The exhibits stressed science and industry of the future. The symbol of the fair was the Trylon and Perisphere to represent the world's upward reach to better living. Inside the 180-foot-diameter Perisphere the visitor saw "Democracity," which was "a dramatic and splendidly

127. Art and beauty as reflected in the souvenirs of the 1939 San Francisco Fair. The 12½″ long hand mirror has a postcard on its topside. One compact is plastic, one metal. The 10½″ plate shows on the reverse "Official Souvenir" made by Homer Laughlin, U.S.A.

executed vision of a city, coordinated and coherent in plan with its surrounding territory, its nearby villages, and neighboring towns." The visitor gazed down onto the model city and landscape from a moving platform circling the inside of the building from which, during the six-minute trip, "Democracity" went through a day from dawn to dusk, depicting what "The World of Tomorrow" would be like.

Most major corporations of America had pavilions or exhibits. You could have taken a ride in a Ford motor car over a specially constructed cork-and-rubber surfaced "Road of Tomorrow," or been selected at the AT&T pavilion to call anyone you chose in the United States—free. That is, as long as you didn't mind other visitors with headsets listening in on your conversation.

Sixty-three foreign nations had pavilions or exhibits.

The fair attracted more than 45 million visitors during the April-to-October periods it ran each year, but it was not able to make a profit.

There were fifty stands operated by the Exposition Souvenir Corporation, the official concessionaire for souvenirs and novelties. In addition, exhibitors sold or gave away items of a souvenir nature. The illustrations in Plates 128, 129, and 130 show a range of this fair's souvenirs and the utilitarian nature of some of them.

128. A collection of some of the housewares produced in "Porcelier" with hand-painted Trylon and Peri-sphere for the New York 1939 Fair. Tall pot is 6½".

129. A collection of items from the New York 1939 Fair. Counterclockwise from top left: pencil flashlight key ring, postcard charm brace-let, assorted buttons/badges from commercial companies as well as the U.S.S.R. The salt-and-pepper set was made of plastic and came in many colors.

130. World's Fair dining in style. The 10½" plate was made for Tiffany by Adams Brothers, the glass was prob-ably made by Libby, and the silverware is marked William Rogers International Silver . . . all set on a World's Fair tablecloth.

131. An unmarked 4″ dish with the symbol of Seattle's World's Fair, 1962.

SEATTLE, WASHINGTON, 1962

After more than a 20-year gap, the first post-war international fair in North America opened on April 21, 1962, in Seattle. Its official name was "Century 21 Exposition," and its theme was "A preview of life in the next century," as well as man in the space age.

The symbol of the fair was the 600-foot-high Space Needle, which was topped by a squat dish-shaped structure housing an observation deck, lounge, and restaurant as illustrated on the small plate shown in Plate 131. The visitor rode up in a glass-fronted capsule elevator. The lounge featured a cocktail called the "Space Needle," which was served in a glass in the shape of the structure. If you had more than one of these and were ready to swear that the world was spinning before your eyes, you would have been right if you consider spinning to be one revolution an hour. The structure turned so that the visitor saw Puget Sound and the Cascade and Olympic mountains, to say nothing of Seattle and the fair, slowly pass before his eyes.

A transportation feature of the fair was the monorail system which carried passengers the 1.2 miles from downtown Seattle to the fair in 96 seconds. The cars were silent, featured large windows, and the supports and rails on which the cars rode were not unduly cumbersome or scarring to the landscape.

The Century 21 Exposition had exhibits from forty-eight different nations, attracted some ten million visitors during its six-month run, and was a financial success.

NEW YORK WORLD'S FAIR, 1964–1965

This fair was plagued by general public apathy, slow construction, and denial of official recognition as a World's Fair by the Bureau of International Expositions, which probably reduced participation by foreign countries, or at least their level of expenditure.

The theme of the fair was "Man's achievements on a shrinking globe in an expanding universe," and it had as its symbol the 120-foot-wide stainless-steel globe called Unisphere. That symbol still stands in lonesome grandeur close to the Grand Central Parkway, Van Wyck Expressway, and the Long Island Expressway, mocking "man's achievements" in the daily crawl of autos on the congested highways leading from the city to the suburbs.

Arts and entertainment covered a wide spectrum at the fair, as did the souvenirs, as shown in Plates 132 and 133. For more sacred themes, there was Michelangelo's *Pietà* in the Italian Pavilion, blessed by Pope Paul VI during his personal visit to the fair. There were also some dazzling pavilions provided by American industry. At the IBM Building you entered what looked like grandstand bleachers for a football game. Then, when filled, the whole bleacher with its load of spectators took off—rising some 90 feet skyward into a white egg-shaped structure where you viewed America on many movie screens all in action at once, or in quick eye-blinking sequence. At GE's Carrousel Theatre there were four stage settings showing the story of electricity in the American home: at the turn of the century, in the 1920s, in the 1940s, and tomorrow. But rather than do it the easy way and have the stage rotate, the entire theater with audience seated in it went around the four settings and then finally discharged the visitor through a hole in the middle of the stage.

However, the fair was not financially successful and paid something less than twenty cents on the dollar to its backers.

132. From the New York World's Fair of 1964–1965: beer tray, 6¾″ frosted glasses, a charm bracelet, and a metal replica of the Unisphere.

133. For the younger generation at the 1964–1965 New York World's Fair there was the 13″ bendable "Miss New York" doll, or the Milton Bradley game sold in its self-contained mailing envelope.

EXPO '67, MONTREAL, CANADA

Officially called "Universal and International Exposition of 1967," but known as EXPO '67, it had as its theme "Man and His World." The fair was built on a man-made island in the St. Lawrence River and was composed of 166 buildings in which 62 nations were represented. This fair excelled in architecture and design, and many bold new ideas were presented.

Among the outstanding buildings were the Labyrinth, "a modern maze of contrast, paradoxes, and multiple dimensions," and Safdie's Habitat. This was 158 flats arranged in 20 different groupings on 12 different levels. Each unit was constructed from a prefab model unit 38′ × 17′ × 10′. The structure looked like a stack of uneven and unbalanced toy blocks, but it was actually a rational and well-thought-out answer to the need for privacy and variety in a mass-produced, congested world. Canada's own national exhibit was housed in an inverted pyramid shown on the stamps in the accompanying illustration (Plate 134).

Fifty million people came to the fair, and it was so successful that it has continued to open each year as "Man and His World." Canada had the forethought to ask the nations to turn the structures over to Montreal rather than tear them down. The United States Building, a steel and plastic geodesic dome created by Buckminster Fuller, is now holding forth as a huge bird cage.

134. Souvenirs were sold at locations other than the Fair itself, as suggested by the Macy's tie-in for Montreal's EXPO 67. The stamps and pencil are Canadian, the medal was issued by the United Nations, and the badges show the then new Canadian flag, the symbol of the Fair, and a U.S.S.R. pin.

HEMISFAIR '68, SAN ANTONIO, TEXAS

Immediately after EXPO '67, the fairgoer could have headed south to visit Hemisfair '68, which stressed, as its name implied, this hemisphere. While earlier fairs had been constructed on land-fill, swamps, or man-created islands, the Texas fair employed a true urban twentieth-century concept. It was built on 92 acres of downtown space that had been cleared of its slums and was only two blocks from the Alamo.

The fair attracted nineteen foreign nations and fifteen industrial corporations. Once again the dominant feature was a tower structure named the "Tower of the Americas," as shown on the souvenir tray in Plate 135. The fair drew some six million people during its six-month run but was not financially successful. However, it left San Antonio with not only a park with a lake in the middle of the city, but a convention hall, arena, and theater. Not bad planning at all on the part of those Texans.

EXPO '74, SPOKANE, WASHINGTON

The International Exposition on the Environment was held in Spokane from May through October 1974. This fair has been called "the quiet fair" for there was not much promotion or publicity, but that is what the promoters said was their aim: to make it more regional than international. It did attract more than five million visitors and had as its theme that man must live in harmony with nature.

BICENTENNIAL 1976

At first, discussions about celebrating the nation's 200th anniversary centered about the selection of a theme and location for a great exposition. Boston, New York, Philadelphia, and Washington, D.C., were among the cities that expressed interest in hosting the celebration. Pennsylvania proclaimed itself the "Bicentennial State" on its auto license plates.

But then decentralization won increasing support. Let every state, city, and community hold its own celebration in a manner each considered appropriate. The resulting diversity meant a bonanza in the souvenir field. Thousands of items have been marketed in honor of, in support of, and in the name of the United States Bicentennial, in unlimited styles, and at all levels of price. Just one example of this mass outpouring is shown (Plate 136).

135. San Antonio's 1968 World's Fair shows its international flavor in this 10¾" lacquer tray made in Japan.

136. A look forward, a glance backward is reflected in this 3¾" mug produced in the United States for the Bicentennial.

Mention should also be made of the U.S. Bicentennial Society which established itself in 1973 as a private corporation to "assure the existence of valuable commemorative objects worthy of our nation's bicentennial celebration." It adopted the symbol of the double eagle and the motto, "Pride in the past, strength for the future." This Society sold its seal of approval to products and dealers.

WORLD'S FAIR SOUVENIRS

The illustrations in this section give only a small sample of the souvenirs collected from world's fairs. Here is a short—and not complete—listing of categories of souvenirs which have come to be collected:

CERAMIC, GLASS, METAL, TEXTILE

Ash trays
Banks
Beer mugs
Buttons and badges
Charms
Coins and medals
Dishes
Dolls
Fans
Figurines
Flags and pennants
Glasses
Handkerchiefs and scarfs
Hats and clothes items
Household items
Jewelry
Leather goods
Matchsafes
Mirrors
Models
Pens and pencils
Pillows
Pins
Plates and plaques
Ribbons
Sewing items
Spoons
Tokens
Toys
Trays
Wooden nickels and elongated coins

PAPER

Advertisements
Books
Catalogues
Exhibit material and literature
Maps
Matches
Menus
News releases
Pamphlets, folders, and booklets
Pictures
Plans
Playing cards
Postcards
Programs
Seals and decals
Slides and movies
Stamps
Tickets

Part III

Other
Pictorial
Souvenirs

The field of souvenirs is huge. The discussion to this point has covered only two rather small areas: ceramic pictorials and those souvenirs associated with world's fairs and expositions held in North America. There still is an immense range of wares in the souvenir field, even when limited to those bearing a pictorial representation. As a result, we have had to impose some rather arbitrary and, perhaps from certain viewpoints, narrow-minded judgments as to which additional items to cover.

The criteria for inclusion have been those governing the ceramic part of the book: the item carries a pictorial view, or at the minimum the name of the place with the legend, "Souvenir of . . ." The items to be discussed should also be available in reasonably good quantity, and at inexpensive to moderate price levels. Even with these restrictions, we recognize that there are other wares which might have been included.

For example, there is no coverage of textiles, although some types certainly fall within the souvenir pictorial field: scarfs, handkerchiefs, pennants, badges, items in the apparel field, from T-shirts to hats. Other materials not covered here include wood, leather, plastic, and some items of metal or glass.

But enough of what has been omitted. What follows is a summary of other items in the pictorial souvenir field with which you can satisfy your souvenir instinct when next you visit a flea market or antique show.

POSTCARDS

The picture postcard is the universal souvenir. It is the one that is bought in all places by everyone, even by those who otherwise never indulge the souvenir instinct. It is the largest seller, by far, of any souvenir, and is found in spots that carry no other souvenir items. And postcards are collected—by the thousands, in numbers bought and traded, and in the number of individuals who are collectors.

The postcard's history is closely related to other wares in the souvenir field. Many pictorial souvenir wares used the view from a postcard for the art work on a ceramic or metal item.

As a separate piece and style of mail, the postcard dates back to Europe and about 1869. The first official postal card in the United States was issued by the Post Office Department in 1873 for one penny. You wrote your message on one side, and the address on the other, as you do today on the official postal cards still used by the post office.

During the late 1800s, advertising or greetings (Christmas and New Year) appeared on postal cards which had drawings or art work on them. But all had the address—and the address alone—on one side, and the message on the other. Private publishers were permitted to produce cards as long as they left the address side alone. If there was a picture, the message had to be on the side with the view. In some cards the picture covered only part of the space so a message could be added, or you simply wrote over the picture. The late 1890s saw a flood of postal cards with views, in colors, and in many styles, such as comic, novelty, or what we today would call "questionable taste." Most were printed in Germany but carried the phrase "Published by" and the name of an American merchant. A. C. Bosselman & Co., which was also a distributor of ceramics, published postcards, or postal cards as they were officially called until December 24, 1901, when the Post Office permitted the shorter term to be used on privately published cards. But that was a name change only. Postcards in the form we know did not arrive until 1907.

Postal regulations were changed as of March 1, 1907, to permit the picture to occupy one side, and the message and address the other. If you have any old postcards and they have the address space and message space on the same side, you can be sure they are no older than 1907.

Plate 137 shows another use for the postcard. It was placed under glass and inside a light metal frame to form a pin tray or coaster.

137. Metal tray with postcard view under glass of Atlantic City's Beach. 5½" x 3½".

RUBY GLASS

Souvenirs made from ruby glass began to be produced just before the beginning of this century. Ruby glass is pressed glass in which the red color is obtained by "flashing," or staining part of the piece with a red tint (a much cheaper process than producing true colored glass). Generally the words "Souvenir of . . ." are blocked or etched onto the piece, plus the name of the place or event, and sometimes a date. The wares were mass-produced and not expensive, making them ideal as souvenirs.

Ruby glass souvenirs were offered at the World's Columbian Exposition in Chicago in 1893, but many more examples can be found from the St. Louis Exposition of 1904. These dated pieces (Plate 138) indicate how this style of souvenir grew in popularity at the beginning of this century.

138. St. Louis Exposition 1904 ruby glass souvenir items. Tumbler is 4" high. *Courtesy of Mrs. Ruth Olsen.*

139. Two mugs and small pitcher in ruby glass. Utica mug is 3¼″ high. Note the different glass patterns.

140. Additional items made in ruby glass for the souvenir trade. The Atlantic City mug is 3½″ high. *Courtesy of Mrs. Ruth Olsen.*

The use of ruby glass was not limited to fairs and expositions. Ruby glass has been produced throughout this century. Katharine M. Mc-Clinton in her book *Antiques, Past and Present* says the production of souvenir ruby glass items expanded to include "almost every American town and state [being] represented by an inscribed name and date." Regretfully, from the collector's viewpoint, some of the items being made today suggest by their dates that they were made much earlier. An example is a small pitcher with the inscription "Gettysburg 1863." It most certainly is not that old, but it can, with justice, be sold as a souvenir of the Civil War battle of that date as long as the buyer is aware that it is a modern souvenir rather than an antique. Once you have handled a number of ruby glass items, it is possible to tell from the feel of the glass an old example from a more modern one.

Mrs. McClinton in her discussion of ruby glass souvenirs says that at the turn of this century most were made in Pittsburgh. Some of the firms she lists are: Adams & Co.; Doyle & Co.; U.S. Glass Co.; Model Glass Works; Pioneer Glass Co.; Fostoria Glass Co.; Richard and Hartley; and George Duncan & Sons. A wide range of examples can still be found at shops and antique shows.

All of the pieces in the first illustration are from the St. Louis Exposition of 1904. Although several different patterns of pressed glass were used for the souvenirs, the so-called button arches found in these examples were the most common. The other illustrations, Plates 139 and 140, show the kind of towns and places represented on ruby glass and the different patterns used for the wares. Utica and Schenectady have thumbnail patterns, the Atlantic City mug carries a flower design, and the Shelbourne Falls piece is designed like a beer stein. The small item from Blue Ball shows the continued popularity of ruby glass souvenirs, for this colorfully named town in the Pennsylvania Dutch region has become a tourist area only since the 1950s.

GLASS PAPERWEIGHTS

Scenic glass paperweights are the poor cousins in the glass paperweight field. No Baccarat, Clichy, or St. Louis millefiori these, but simply shapes that capture a scene under glass. Souvenir glass paperweights were primarily a Victorian ornament which came into fashion at the beginning of the century. They were produced in huge quantities, and many were used by tradesmen as promotional or giveaway items, as well as sold as souvenirs. They were also used as a forerunner of the church plate, for many are found with a view of the local church, sometimes with the minister shown in a small photograph.

They come in a variety of shapes, but the most common is rectangular with rounded edges about 4″ long by 2½″ across. Some have a smooth, others a ruffled under edge. Some are round or octagonal, and some have a dome shape like their more elegant cousins, but generally these Victorian paperweights are flat on top. All have weight to the glass, and you know you have picked up something capable of performing its utilitarian task. The picture is affixed to the bottom, looking up through the glass. Frequently the backing, or matting, will show the name of the merchant or distributor who handled the piece. The picture will generally be a photograph, although some are hand-painted or tinted. Today some of these paperweights have been "redone" by inserting a new picture. But these can be recognized either by the style of the picture or by the workmanship in pasting the piece to the bottom.

A. C. Bosselman & Co., a New York wholesaler mentioned earlier, was also involved in glass paperweights and had the habit of adding its name and address to the wares distributed. Because the firm changed addresses frequently, its wares can be dated both by the view and the address shown. A. C. Bosselman's New York addresses were:

1904:	469 Broadway
1912:	114 East 16th Street
1915:	3 East 13th Street
1918:	248 Lafayette Street
1926:	164 Fifth Avenue

141. Victorian glass paperweights. East Windham, New York; Dancing Pavilion, Virginia Beach. Both 2½″ x 4″ and distributed by A. C. Bosselman & Co.

142. Selection of styles and shapes of glass paperweights. The large weight of Newport is 7″ x 4″. L to R, top to bottom: Breakers Mansion, Newport, R.I.; School, Fredericton, N.B.; Bathing Beach, Newport, R.I.; Church, Alexandria, Va.; Gettysburg, Pa.

The two weights illustrated in Plate 141 carry the Bosselman name. The one of East Windham has the address 469 Broadway, while the Dancing Pavilion of Virginia Beach shows 114 East 16th Street.

The pictures on paperweights (see Plate 142) may occasionally have been designed specifically for them, but more likely they came from postcards which were cut to fit the bottom of the glass. Remember that Bosselman was also a "Publisher" of postcards. That firm was one of the first to serve all areas of the souvenir trade.

These paperweights are not expensive as yet. Prices range from about five to fifteen dollars, depending on scene, shape, and condition. Some do command higher prices and are beginning to appear at antique shows.

METAL FORMS

Wares in the shape of the building or structure were made of inexpensive metal-based material and date primarily from before the 1940s. They were produced in Japan. Some souvenirs were produced simply as a representation of the structure. Others had additional uses, such as pencil sharpeners, banks, or receptacles for keys, coins, or stamps.

Frequently a particular structure would be produced in several different sizes. Older forms show that a good degree of care was taken in the production of the mold. Some have value as works of popular art. However, more recent ones have been made of plastic or a light alloy and have a minimum of detail. All of the examples shown in Plate 143 are pre-1940s and were made in Japan.

143. Metal souvenir sculptures made in Japan. L to R: Statue of Liberty; The Capitol, Washington, D.C.; the Empire State Building; and the White House.

METAL RELIEF VIEWS

Another mass-produced metal souvenir was the pressed or cast metal object which showed a local view in relief. These were also made in Japan during the 1920s and 1930s and were sold to local merchants by the same jobbers who sold them ceramic pictorial souvenirs. Once again the source of the views was the postcard.

Sales literature of John H. Roth & Co. from 1926 to 1930 reveals the wholesale prices of these metal souvenirs. Roth's pattern books for "metal souvenirs, trays, boxes and novelties" show that these wares were "especially popular with the seaside and mountain resorts." The prices quoted included the cost of making the molds. Orders took from eight months to a year for delivery.

In 1930, for items such as those illustrated in Plate 144, the prices were:

Crumb tray with scraper, with 3 or 4 views, gilt
and silver: 5½″ × 5¾″
  18 doz. order: $12.80 per doz.
  24 "   "   :   10.00 "   "
  36 "   "   :   9.00 "   "

Pin tray with one large view in center, gilt and
silver oxidized floral border:
  36 doz. order: $ 3.80 per doz.
  60 "   "   :   3.45 "   "
  100 "   "   :   3.15 "   "

Ash tray with one view in middle and three
views on rim, gilt and silver:
  36 doz. order: $ 3.10 per doz.
  60 "   "   :   2.75 "   "
  100 "   "   :   2.40 "   "

These were never expensive to produce or sell. Today frequently these metal souvenirs are not found in good shape, as the metal is soft and tends to bend and corrode, giving the surface a blurred, tarnished look. Items found on the antique market today are still close to their original prices. The crumb tray, for example, which wholesaled for about one dollar in the 1930s, commands only a few dollars more almost half a century later.

Once again, as with the ceramics, the views are what make these wares interesting and help in determining when a particular item was first produced. Look at the items showing New York City with the

144. Metal relief forms made in Japan with views of cities. The long middle tray is 8½" x 3". L to R, top to bottom: "Souvenir of Harrisburg, Pa." (Capitol upper center, Soldiers Monument, middle); "Souvenir of New York" (Woolworth Building and Statue of Liberty); "New State Capitol Building, Richmond, Va."; "Souvenir of New York" (with Brooklyn Bridge in middle); "Souvenir of Atlantic City, N.J." (Beachfront showing Marlborough and Traymore Hotels).

Flatiron Building (1902) and the Woolworth Building (1913) as the major structures of interest. Since new structures were added as quickly as possible, these items surely were produced pre-1932, the year the Empire State Building came to dominate the New York City souvenir field as well as the skyline.

SOUVENIR SPOONS

The collecting of souvenir spoons started in the late 1880s as a fad which quickly grew into a major mania. Any matron traveling in the 1890s was almost certain to return with souvenir spoons for her best friends, to say nothing of adding several spoons to her own collection.

Some of the first spoons were fairly plain, with simply the name of the city on the handle. But soon distinctive handles, relief pictures, raised letters, cutout forms, and the ornate Victorian influence were found on many spoons. Naturally silver makers and merchants were delighted with the popularity of the souvenir spoon. Gorham was one of the earliest to produce many different designs of sterling souvenir spoons. By 1891 a book had been published by George B. James in which more than 2,000 souvenir spoons are mentioned.

Towns, cities, states, buildings, events, and people were all subjects of souvenir spoons. Frequently the same spoon was made in several forms to make "Madam's" decision a little more difficult. David Low of Salem, Massachusetts, in 1891 produced a Lexington spoon available in:

Teaspoon	$2.00
Teaspoon, with gold bowl	2.50
Orange Spoon	2.25
Orange Spoon, with gold bowl	2.50
Coffee Spoon	1.25
Coffee Spoon, with gold bowl	1.50

In some ways the souvenir spoon may be the most popular of any souvenir item, for it is easy to transport, reasonably indestructible, both usable and decorative, and finally, still inexpensive per individual piece, ranging in price from about ten to fifteen dollars. Some command higher prices, and prices have been rising both from the continued popularity of this article and the fact that silver itself has appreciated in price during the past decade.

The illustrations in Plates 145 and 146 show a representative sample of North American souvenir spoons. But as any traveler knows, this is not an American field only. Almost every city and every nation has its own range of souvenir spoons for the true Spooner to collect.

Of the spoons illustrated in Plate 145, the Statue of Liberty is by Tiffany and has a gold dusted bowl. It was first introduced in Tiffany's Blue Book of 1891. The Hawaii spoon of Pele, Goddess of Fire, was patented by Gorham in 1894. In Plate 146 the small coffee spoon of the Chicago 1893 Exposition was the official World's Fair spoon. It shows Columbus on the handle, his ship in relief in the bowl, and a picture of Queen Isabella on the reverse. It was designed by Alvin Beiderhase & Co., New York, for B. F. Norris, Alister & Co., Chicago, and sold at the fair for $1.25. The teaspoon of the same design was originally priced at $2.

145. Selection of souvenir spoons, all approx. 5½" long. L to R, top to bottom: Texas; New Orleans; Pittsburgh; Utah; Statue of Liberty; Atlantic City; Hawaii; Seattle; Sacramento; and Mount Vernon. *Courtesy of Frances Broughton.*

146. Souvenir spoons with figures or forms in the handle, and three coffee spoons. Spoons top row 5½" to 6¼" long, coffee spoons 4" long. L to R, top to bottom: Pueblo Indian of New Mexico; Omaha Indian; Montreal; Texas; Florida; official spoon of the Columbian Exposition, Chicago, 1893; Denver, Colorado; and Bridgehampton, New York. *Courtesy of Frances Broughton.*

Part IV

Souvenirs Today

Within the trade, souvenirs in the past have always been termed a one-coin operation. That is, items were marketed so that they could be paid for by one coin. That "coin" went from the dime at the start of the century, to the quarter, and then the half-dollar. But in recent years two factors have killed this one-coin tradition: inflation, and that now all but universal dredge called a sales tax. So that even if an item is marked at a round figure, the addition of the sales tax causes a few pennies to be added.

Although the price of souvenirs has gone up over the years, they still represent—compared to other expenditures of today—a moderate outlay. They can be purchased on the spur of the moment without a major dent in the budget. A representative sample of items in the pictorial souvenir field on display in the Empire State Building in New York showed that prices ranged from $.98 to $4.98 (plus tax). Postcards were lower and jewelry was higher.

Some pictorial souvenirs today present scenes that cover a wider geographic area than souvenirs did in the past. Examples are the baked clay wall hanging plaque showing the Pikes Peak Region (Plate 147) and the two state plates of Texas and Washington (Plate 148). The

Texas plate was made by a decal process, now widely used for pictorial wares.

These wares, like most pictorial souvenirs today, are bought and collected to be displayed on a child's room wall or in the family den or recreation room to show where the family has traveled. Some of the newer pictorial souvenirs appeal to the driver and show the roads over which the trip was made, such as the Illinois Tollway illustrated in Plate 149—a true pictorial souvenir of today.

One other comparatively recent entry follows an old tradition. The entire field had its start in the inexpensive items sold at county fairs and carnivals. Today pictorial souvenirs are found at safari parks, children's playgrounds, zoos, historical craft and restoration sites, but the largest playgrounds for all ages are the two Walt Disney creations. The horse-drawn car shown in Plate 150 is the perfect symbol with which to conclude this trip. Whether old or young, we keep rolling along, and sometimes it is a delight to return to the past, perhaps through the memory associated with a view on a pictorial souvenir.

147. Pressed clay molded wall hanging showing scenes of "Pikes Peak Region." 12″ x 10½″.

148. Two modern state plates, both made in the United States. The 9″ Texas plate was made by a decal process. The Washington 9½″ plate is a medium green transfer print.

149. Multicolored 9″ plate of "Illinois Toll-way." Made in Japan.

150. "Walt Disney World" showing a horse-drawn streetcar. 8″ heavy green glaze, brown center, dish or plaque.

Selected
Bibliography

Altman, Seymour and Violet. *The Book of Buffalo Pottery*. New York: Crown, 1969.

Barber, Edwin Atlee. *Marks of American Potters*. Southhampton, N.Y.: Cracker Barrel Press.

Cole, Ann Kilborn. *How to Collect the "New" Antiques*. New York: David McKay Co., 1966.

Connelly, John. *A Century of Uninterrupted Progress*. Boston: Geo. H. Ellis Co., 1910.

Coysh, William. *Blue and White Transfer Ware, 1780–1840*. Rutland, Vt.: Tuttle, 1970.

———. *Blue-Printed Earthenware 1800–1850*. Rutland, Vt.: Tuttle, 1972.

Cushion, J. P. *Pocket Book of German Ceramic Marks*. London: Faber and Faber, Ltd., 1961.

Gabriel, Juri. *Victorian Furniture and Furnishings*. New York: Grosset & Dunlap, 1971.

Godden, G. A. *Encyclopaedia of British Pottery and Porcelain Marks*. New York: Crown, 1964.

Gores, Stan. *1876 Centennial*. Fond du Lac, Wisc.: Haber Printing Co., 1974.

Henderson, Ian. *Pictorial Souvenirs of Britain*. London: David & Charles, 1974.

Klamkin, Marian. *American Patriotic and Political China*. New York: Scribner's, 1973.

Laidacker, Sam. *Anglo-American China* (Parts I & II). Bristol, Pa.: Sam Laidacker, 1954.

Larsen, Elouise Baker. *American Views on Staffordshire*. New York: Dover, 1975.

Little, W. L. *Staffordshire Blue*. New York: Crown, 1969.

McClinton, Katharine Morrison. *Antiques, Past and Present*. New York: Clarkson N. Potter, Inc., 1971.

———. *The Complete Book of Small Antiques Collecting*. New York: Bramhall House, 1965.

Mebane, John. *Collecting Nostalgia*. New York: Popular Library, 1966.

Ray, Marcia. *Collectible Ceramics*. New York: Crown, 1974.

Staff, Frank. *The Picture Postcard and Its Origins*. New York: Praeger, 1966.

Stefano, Frank. *Check-List of "Wedgwood Old Blue Historical Plates" and Other Views of U.S.A. Imported by Jones, McDuffee & Stratton*. Privately printed, July 1975.

Index

(*Illustrations are indicated by italic numbers*)